ADVANCE PRAISE

"One of the great joys of serving as U.S. Ambassador to the Russian Federation was working with General Peter Zwack. Every day, he demonstrated a deep commitment both to serving our great nation and to understanding Russia. The latter helped him do the former. *Swimming the Volga** shows just how deep into Russian society, history, and culture Peter dug. Jumping from the analytic to the personal with ease, it's a brilliant story."

—AMBASSADOR MICHAEL MCFAUL
U.S. Ambassador to Russia 2012-2014
Author of *Cold War, Hot Peace; An American Ambassador in Putin's Russia*

"Loaded with great insights and stories from his days before serving as U.S. Defense Attaché in Moscow and from his deep involvement with Russia, Brigadier General Zwack brings the past alive to help us understand what Putin is doing today. It is very rare to have pages filled by someone who really knows Russia and knows how to write about it."

—LESLIE H. GELB
President Emeritus, Council on Foreign Relations

**Swimming the Volga* is a lively, short memoir of life in the small Russian city of Tver (110m from Moscow) as seen through the eyes of a young captain in the U.S. Army during a summer program on Russian culture and language in 1989.

"Over a ten- year period, Zwack continued his visits to Tver, even as he rose in rank and responsibility. In return, the city provided him with a unique window into the upheavals of Russia in the 1990s. Through Zwack's stories, we meet a set of Russian friends he met at the start of the difficult days in the Soviet Union, through the changes of today's Russia in their lives—as well as the eternal characteristics of the Russian people. An informative and entertaining account by an unusually perceptive visitor."

—SUZANNE MASSIE
Personal advisor on the U.S.S.R. to President Ronald Reagan
Author of "Land of the Firebird:" The Beauty of Old Russia and Trust but Verify: Reagan, Russia, and Me - a memoir of the years 1984-1988

"This warm and evocative memoir of a Russia addled by change post-1989 is a remarkable chronicle of a U.S. Army officer's disarming empathy for the young Russians he befriended as they sought to find their place in a new world. Never judgmental, the author captures the rich humanity of the successes and failures of unlikely friends and acquaintances observed during the tumultuous decade between Gorbachev and Putin. Moving and haunting."

—RALPH PETERS
Author of Red Army, Cain at Gettysburg and Looking for Trouble

"This 'coming of age as a Russian Foreign Area Officer' memoir is a phenomenal, warm and provocative story told by retired Brigadier Peter Zwack. Peter and I are friends and fellow soldiers; we served together in Germany during the Cold War and I was honored to observe his magnificent performance as the Defense Attaché in Moscow during the start of what is now the 'hot peace.' During the years in between, Peter's professional demeanor, Russian acumen, and informed insight evolved, in part, as he swam the Volga every summer for a decade. This work provides unique understanding of that part of the world."

—**Lt. General Mark Hertling (Ret)**
Former Commander U.S. Army Europe
Author of *Growing Physician Leaders*
CNN national security and military analyst

"Few Americans understand Russians better than Peter Zwack. As a traveler, student, observer and head military attaché to Moscow, he has come to know them in the many aspects of their lives. This memoir, seen through the prism of Zwack's experiences with the people of one city, Tver, is a sharp-eyed view of a complex, contradictory and—yes, extraordinary—nation."

Robert Cowley
Founding Editor, MHQ: The Quarterly Journal of Military History Author of the upcoming *The Killing Season*

SWIMMING

THE

VOLGA

SWIMMING

THE

VOLGA

A U.S. Army Officer's Experiences

in

Pre-Putin Russia

1989-1999

AN UNPUBLISHED MEMOIR

TEN YEARS VISITING TVER

BRIGADIER GENERAL PETER B. ZWACK {RET}

FORMER U.S. DEFENSE ATTACHÉ TO THE RUSSIAN FEDERATION

Swimming the Volga

Brigadier General Peter B. Zwack (Ret)
U.S. Defense Attaché to the Russian Federation 2012–2014
Woodrow Wilson Center Global Fellow, The Kennan Institute

First Edition

ISBN: 978-1-7340060-1-8 (Paperback)
ISBN: 978-1-7340060-0-1 (Hardcover)
ISBN: 978-1-7340060-9-4 (Large Print)
ISBN: 978-1-7340060-2-5 (ePub)
ISBN: 978-1-7340060-8-7 (Audio Book)

Library of Congress Control Number: 2019913172

Zwack Eurasia Consultancy LLC

All photos are courtesy of the author unless otherwise indicated.

https://PeterBZwack.net

Dedication

To my parents - Iris Rogers Argento and Peter Zwack, Sr. - who inspired my lifelong fascination with Russia and greater Eurasia.

TABLE OF CONTENTS

FOREWORD

ONE OF RUSSIA'S BEST-KNOWN NINETEENTH-CENTURY writers, Ivan Turgenev, made his name with a series of sharp-eyed sketches of village life published under the title *Notes of a Hunter.*

Like Turgenev, U.S. Brigadier General Peter B. Zwack is also a keen observer of life in Russia, a country which he has experienced as a military man, academic and frequent visitor to the ancient northern Russian city of Tver. He has seen the city, and its people, in bad times and in good, first during the Soviet Union era and now in the New Russia.

In this personal memoir, Peter Zwack takes us into the lives of ordinary Russians swept up in the fascinating chaos of tumultuous political, economic and social transition between 1989 and 1999. Fluent in the nuances of the Russian language, he is both observer and participant, capturing the excitement, the dread, the fears, the dreams of his Russian friends and acquaintances. Epic change can sometimes best be revealed in personal details and stories, like the 'entrepreneur' who "still keeps a shotgun by his desk and a large Doberman on the premises." Or the old man on a train who told Zwack he was "voting for his grandchildren's future."

Peter Zwack comes from adventurous stock – his mother met her second husband on the Trans-Siberian railroad. His father, a scion of the famous Hungarian Unicum distillery, fled with his parents to the West, carrying the digestif secret formula with them.

One of the first Americans that Tver residents had ever encountered, Zwack soon struck up casual friendships with some of the locals, who were happy to introduce their new American friend to their world. He returned several times between 1989 and 1999—a period during which his friends, Tver and the old U.S.S.R. underwent unprecedented change.

After his 1999 visit, Zwack never thought he would return to Tver, but in 2012 he made the trip again—this time as a Brigadier General, the Senior U.S. Defense Official and Attaché to Russia.

His Tver friends were then in their 40's; some had disappeared, some had died, some were prospering in new jobs or new businesses. The old Russia he had experienced first-hand in the

1990s had moved on. The new Russia (to which he returned yet again in 2017) now lives "in the world of existential threats, real, perceived and, also very importantly," he says, "contrived in a way that is very hard for those of us in the U.S. and West to fully understand."

By sharing his personal experiences three decades ago in the quintessentially Russian town of Tver, Peter Zwack helps us grasp the Russia of today.

—JILL DOUGHERTY

Former CNN Moscow Bureau Chief and deep expert on Russia and the Soviet Union.

Jill Dougherty is a journalist, anchor, and correspondent. She worked as an anchor and foreign affairs correspondent for CNN for over three decades. Based in Hong Kong and Russia, she was the U.S. Affairs Editor for CNN International and Managing Editor of CNN International Asia/Pacific. In 1993, her team won the 1993 American Journalism Review for best White House Coverage. On occasion, she still reports on Russia for CNN. Slavic and Russian studies at the University of Michigan, Georgetown and Leningrad State University.

A DIFFERENT DRUMMER

"The Full Peter"

—Colonel Tom Wilhelm

Written by Colonel (ret) Tom Wilhelm for Peter's 50th birthday 'roast' in 2004. Col. Wilhelm also participated in a Russian study program in a Soviet city – Leningrad – in summer 1989. He has an illustrious history initially out of West Point serving as a young infantry officer, working direct liaison with the Russians in 1995 Bosnia and serving twice as a Defense Attaché, both in Tajikistan and Mongolia. It was of his extraordinary stint in Ulan Bator, of which distinguished author Robert Kaplan wrote a <u>March 2004</u> Atlantic Monthly article about him titled "The Man who would be Khan."

I met Peter Zwack on my first day at the U.S. Army Russian Institute (USARI) in Garmisch, Germany. This was back in those heady days of 1989. We were sitting in a waiting area outside the USARI Commandant's office, having just arrived that day and being a couple of months (fashionably) late for the start of the two-year program.

Both of us had missed the language refresher phase of the USARI program; instead, we had bent a few of the rules and successfully contrived to attend summer terms at universities in the Soviet Union. Both of us had been impressed by our experiences. Both of us had realized major improvements in our language skills. Both of us were considered AWOL by the Commandant.

While we sat waiting for our interview, we discussed our mutual and unique experiences with gusto. I confess that I harbored a darkling concern about the potential interview with the Commandant. I confided this worry to my newfound comrade, Peter. But Peter tut-tutted me. He said, "Oh really, I think once we tell him how wonderful our experience was, and how it can enhance the program here, he'll be excited."

The Commandant's deputy, a meticulously polite man in whose office we were waiting and who had initially asked lots of positive-sounding questions about our time in Russia, cleared his throat: "Well, you should know that the Comm may not see your experience exactly like you do."

I sensed danger.

Peter said, "No, I'm certain he'll applaud our initiative."

I could practically smell doom.

Eventually, we were summoned and took seats in front of the Commandant. The Colonel didn't say: "Well, good to see you two finally made it" or "Glad you guys decided to join our program" or anything that might have admonished-yet-reassured. I recall instead a haranguing with "So you don't think much of our program here" and "You've just started your FAO careers; you don't know what training you need," and "You can't get language training like this anywhere else; you're behind the rest of your classmates."

Now, I am an officer of only modest skills, so part of my long-term career management has included surviving my supervisors. I began to deploy the necessary defenses: sit up, say "Yes, sir," and excuse myself as expeditiously as possible. What I frankly was smelling was the Uniform Code of Military Justice.

Then the most extraordinary thing happened. Peter shifted in the seat next to me and assumed an even more comfortable position. It was the first time I ever actually witnessed someone in a chair sit in a position that could be called 'draped'. I cringed as he began.

"You know, Colonel…." Peter gazed up at the ceiling at this point, summoning his powers of articulation and creating for himself a sense of collegial informality. (While creating for me the feeling that an armed grenade had been dropped and was bobbling around the floor.)

Peter went on. "It really was a superb experience. I am sure this sort of initiative would benefit all Soviet FAOs." He made a gesture with his arm as if to dismiss all other possible arguments.

I looked back and forth between the two of them to see if I had misinterpreted the Colonel: What nuance of the Commandant's character had Peter picked up on that I had not? What professional opportunity did he perceive that I failed to grasp? For a moment, I was prepared to take that next step in officer growth and professional development. I waited, as many of Peter's friends have before and since, to-see-what-would-happen next.

Well, the veins on both sides of the Colonel's neck stuck out and throbbed, and his face turned beet-red, verging on purple. From behind clenched teeth, he uttered, "I ought to give you both an Article Fifteen! Your scores on the DLPT better be Three-Three or you will be in serious trouble."

My attention was now refocused solely on survival; I made to leave, and quickly. Then I experienced what social science refers to as 'The Full Peter'.

Caught halfway between the chair and the door, I froze as Peter responded in an unchanged tone. (He also might have been doing that wave-off thing with his extended arm—I didn't dare look.). "Sir, I apologize that I haven't helped you to grasp this," he said.

"Oh, God," I said to myself. I may have closed my eyes, thinking it would somehow diminish my presence.

"You see, these in-country university programs are the stuff of the future for Soviet FAOs. Certainly, better than any artificial program. (Was Peter really telling the USARI Commandant that his program was artificial?!) I would be happy to write up a proposal for your review. In fact, I don't see why we couldn't get something happening by the end of the year."

Peter smiled. I prayed. The Colonel sputtered, then clamped his jaws shut, and then he did something that I would not have imagined, indeed, would not have hoped for. He left. His own office.

Peter resurrected himself from his drape. "Well, what are you doing for lunch?" he asked, as he collected me and ushered us out of the Comm's office. "Let me show you my favorite Bavarian restaurant."

.

Introduction

In June 1989, during the waning years of the Cold War, I traveled with a group of American college students to the provincial Soviet city of Kalinin, Russia, to spend the summer studying Russian language and culture at the local university. At the time, I was a young U.S. Army Captain in the Foreign Area Officer program. The shifting political winds of the late 1980s allowed me to receive both a Soviet visa and U.S. military permission to dwell for a few weeks in the fading U.S.S.R. I'm grateful to Mikhail Gorbachev and other Soviet reformers, two American Presidents—Ronald Reagan and George Bush, Sr.—and far-sighted European leaders for cultivating an atmosphere of cooperation that made such groundbreaking travel possible.

Soon after settling into our university digs, we encountered Kalininites who were delighted to introduce their exotic visitors to the private side of life in the late Cold War-era U.S.S.R. From raucous midnight ice hockey games at the local arena to leisurely chess matches on the sun-washed banks of the Volga River to adventurous travels on the country's vast transportation web, I had the rare opportunity to experience authentic Russia that summer. After our classes and excursions, we wiled away long evenings sipping street-procured vodka and local beer while earnestly arguing (in my rudimentary Russian) with new friends about the comparative merits and faults of the American and Soviet systems. Conversations inevitably included questions about freedoms taken for granted in the United States. The lively discussions went on for hours, often drifting to the early summer dawn or until the alcohol supply ran out.

I was no stranger to political discussion or Russia, for that matter. My mother, Iris Rogers Argento, was a Russian scholar. She received her Master's Degree from the Russian Institute at Columbia University in the 1950s, in the early days of the Cold War. She often traveled in the U.S.S.R. and Russia in the 1960s up through the 1990s, exploring Russia's three Buddhist Republics (*Buryatia*, *Kalmykia*, and *Tuva*), then later, Russia's Far East. Her trips took her to remote places, far from big urban centers. In 1969, she met her second husband while traveling on the Trans-Siberian Railroad.

Her first husband—my father, Peter Zwack Sr.—had a very different relationship with Russia. He was born in Budapest in 1927, the only son and future scion of Hungary's famous Unicum distillery. As a teenager, he saw the Soviets up close while trapped during the bitter WWII siege of Budapest. Later, when the Communist Hungarian regime nationalized the family distillery in 1948, my father and his parents were forced to flee to the West. Traveling by steamer to U.S. gateway Ellis Island as refugees, they safeguarded the family's prized Unicum *digestif* secret formula for four decades.[1] After the 'Fall of the Wall' in 1989, the family returned to Hungary and miraculously recovered the distillery. (The facility quickly resurrected the Unicum brand and is thriving in 2021.) In 1990, my father was tapped to be the first ambassador to the United States of newly democratic Hungary. He later served as an independent member of the Hungarian parliament. He strongly supported bringing Hungary into the NATO alliance.

At the time of my father's appointment as ambassador, I was a young U.S. Army military intelligence and foreign area officer studying Russian in Germany. This was less than a year after my landmark summer in Kalinin. Perhaps surprisingly, I was able to stay in the army and maintain my security clearance even as my father renounced his coveted U.S. citizenship in a friendly ceremony in U.S. Embassy Budapest.

Following that first eye-opening summer in Kalinin, I returned to the city on my own eight more times between 1989 and 1999. My visits coincided with a period of extraordinary change in the U.S.S.R. After seventy years of tyranny and oppression under a series of iron-fisted regimes, Russia turned away from its failed social and political experiment and took its first steps toward adopting a democratic and free-market system. The dissolution of the Soviet empire under Mikhail Gorbachev took the world by surprise in 1991, followed by a period of turbulence and upheaval under Boris Yeltsin throughout the 1990s. As an American military officer, I had a front-row seat from which to watch my Kalinin friends evolve and cope—some successfully, some not—with seismic shifts in the economy, law, and daily life under *perestroika* (restructuring) and *glasnost* (openness).

During my regular visits to Kalinin—soon renamed Tver—I witnessed firsthand what happens to ordinary people when their world is turned upside down by forces over which they have little or no control. In the Wild West of the 'new' Russia, a few enterprising Russians quickly figured out how to make huge amounts of money—usually illegally. A nascent mafia mastered the art of bringing necessary and desirable goods to market and extracting 'protection' money from new businesses. Most Russians, however, watched their life savings disappear in two massive devaluations of the ruble in the 1990s.

Many of my Tver friends greeted the 1991 dissolution of the U.S.S.R. with giddiness and high hopes but struggled to find their footing. One university woman sought economic security by taking up the life of a 'kept woman' with the Chechen Mafia. Another friend succeeded in starting up a trucking company but always kept a shotgun and guard dog with him in his office. An intelligent and lovely female acquaintance became a customer service manager in Tver for a U.S. dating company that matched American men with Russian women who were desperate to get out of the country. Other friends plugged along in established academic careers, too tired or too wary of risking what little security they had for the unknown. Long used to disappointment, many older Russians simply accepted that real progress would take well beyond their lifetimes. With luck and patience, their grandchildren might benefit someday.

In late 1999, I began writing *Swimming the Volga* as an informal memoir for my family, friends, and peers of what I saw and experienced in Tver during and after the break-up of the U.S.S.R. To my eyes, the small city on the Volga River one hundred and ten miles northwest of Moscow provided a perfect window into the real-life upheaval and dislocation of the late-Gorbachev era and the Yeltsin years. Moscow might have been the center of political action, but provincial Tver was where policy, pragmatism, opportunism, and real-life converged.

Written in the days just before the names Vladimir Putin and Russia became inseparable, *Swimming the Volga* is a time capsule of a remarkable period in world history—one that began with the final chapter of the Cold War and ended with the hijacking of Russia's future by rapacious financiers, pyramid schemers, and a new criminal element, who together set the stage for Putin's ascension to power and with it, a more assertive and revanchist Russia. Along the way, the cast of memorable characters in my story reveal their very human dreams, ambitions, fears, missteps, cynicism, resilience, and disillusionment.

During the three decades since that period of extraordinary political transformation, my own life changed in big ways too. I became deeply and professionally involved with Russia, ultimately rising to the rank of Brigadier General and being appointed our senior U.S. Senior Defense Official and Attache to Russia from 2012 to 2014. I discovered that rereading my diaries about my early visits to Russia provided me with useful nuggets of wisdom and perspective to handle an array of people and issues. My longstanding friendships with the Russians I encountered in Kalinin helped me appreciate the Russian people and their complex, often difficult history, even while I stood firm against Russia's anti-Western policies and actions at home and abroad.

Today, the world is marking the thirtieth anniversary of the extraordinary break-up of the Soviet Union on December 26, 1991—a seismic political event that shook the global order just two years after my stint in Kalinin. The anniversary is a reminder that in a world filled with uncertainties, shifting alliances, and dangerous agendas, it is more important than ever to take the time to engage those who frequently disagree with us. I hope this book's very personal insights into the history, culture, and politics of 1990s Russia will provide the necessary context to more fully understand the enigmatic and often frustrating Russia of 2021. For better or worse, the security and future of our world rest on our willingness to listen and learn.

Note: I've kept the main body of *Swimming the Volga* substantially as it was written in 1999 to best capture—without revisionism—the feel of the time; editing was by and large limited to changes for clarity. I've added an introduction and afterword to bring it into a contemporary context for our turbulent times. The final chapter, "Other Views, Other Voices," showcases the reminisces of six American students and our trip leader who were with me in Tver in 1989. Their varied perspectives complement my own account. I also included two of my "Letters Home" that flesh out my story in real-time.

Tver, Summer 1999

Where were the Antonov air transports? Their familiar bumblebee-like drone was nowhere to be heard.

The question popped into my head while doing a lazy backstroke across the calm, almost current-less waters of the Volga River, Russia's 'Mother of All Rivers.' The huge aircraft were a permanent fixture of summertime Tver, and their distinctive buzzing was one of the customary sounds of early evening along the river. I flipped over to do a slow crawl, occasionally looking down into the deep greenish-brown murk of the polluted river, a sluggish ribbon of water wending its way through provincial Tver, about one hundred and ten miles northwest of Moscow.

The shore patrol, ubiquitous in years past, was also strangely absent. I remembered seeing them for the first time in the summer of 1989—their small launches snappily sporting a small Soviet ensign as they rounded up rogue river-crossers and shepherded them back to shore. Their work then was not police-state activity but rather a safety measure: every so often a large barge, passenger boat or high-speed *Raket* would come cruising down the Volga's center channel.

That same channel was nearly the undoing of me during one memorable swim in 1991, when I was swept under the Old Bridge almost five hundred yards downstream after the Volga was swollen by heavy rains.[2] The banks and shallows of the muddy-brown river remain deceptively calm until one reaches the middle of the water. There I got caught in the swift current and had no choice but to ride the river to the nearest shoreline. Igor and Kseniya, two good friends of mine standing on the riverbank, saw me disappear downstream and feared for my life. My judgment was lacking that day.

Now, here I was, swimming in the Volga again, eight years later, enjoying a chance to cool off. Tver's half-million residents were sweltering in a June 1999 heatwave, with the temperature several times reaching 95 degrees Fahrenheit—stifling for

Russians living without air conditioning. It seemed that almost the entire city's residents lined both banks of the river, splashing about in the shallows to duck the heat.

I noticed that some modern style and taste had penetrated this remote area. Colorful circa late-1990s bathing suits—boxers even—stood out against the pale fish-belly white Russian bodies of early summer—a marked improvement over the horrifying loin-patches and poorly-cut specimens I remembered from 1989. This was also a period when dozens in the Moscow region were drowning every week—mostly drunken men.

The relaxing easy swim allowed my mind to wander back ten years and reflect on my multiple trips to Tver and its evolution from life in the Soviet Union to today's Russia. While I had written about my travels in Russia in letters to close friends, it was this particular summer—1999—when I decided to write about these travels for a wider audience.

Swimming the Volga is one person's view and perspective of complex, contradictory Russia, seen through the prism of a typical provincial, industrial city. It is a chronicle of a Russia far beyond the semi-cosmopolitan centers of Moscow and St.

3

Petersburg. Tver, formerly Kalinin, became my own personal window into the life, psyche, and soul of Russia and its people far from the Kremlin or Hermitage. Since that memorable summer of 1989, I've revisited Tver eight times.

As a thirty-three-year-old U.S. Army military intelligence officer studying to become a Soviet Foreign Area Officer, I was frankly amazed to receive a visa from the Soviets to study for a summer in then-named Kalinin during 1989, and equally surprised that I received permission from my own superiors to do so. Getting clearance to go was not an easy process from a bureaucratic standpoint. My work community, steeped in the mistrust and tension of the ebbing Cold War, was in the throes of adjusting to a non-confrontational relationship with Russia.

I joined a student group organized by Brown University and the University of Rochester, which had managed to develop a summer study program in Kalinin. Having a group of American students studying the Russian language and culture in this old provincial city on the Volga River was an absolute first for secluded Kalinin. The local population was extremely curious and inquisitive about our U.S. presence, so much so that we appeared on the city's local television station and were featured in the local newspaper.

Meeting and developing friendships with the locals was easy. These were the heady days of Gorbachev's *glasnost* and *perestroika*, a time when almost all pre-existing clichés and norms about negative Soviet and U.S. relations were fast evaporating. Within the fading U.S.S.R., 1989 was a time when a newfound ability to publicly express oneself was replacing sullen, heavy adherence to a discredited, bankrupt ideology—one which few Russians believed in anymore. It was an evolutionary, almost revolutionary time, and I was incredibly lucky to be welcomed into an authentic Russian city long insulated from foreigners and news reporters.

Tver itself has a historical pedigree rivaling Moscow's and is older than St. Petersburg. Established in 1182 near the headwaters of the Volga River, it is one of the earliest Russian settlements. Tver vied for power and influence with the other emerging city-states of Novgorod, Pskov, and Moscow. Some Tverites ruefully note that Tver had a fleeting chance to be the pre-eminent power in all Russia. However, those dreams died in 1485 with the decisive victory of the Muscovites at the historically important, but forgotten battle of Bortenovo.[3]

Tver became very important to resurgent, expanding Russia as the Mongol threat faded and European challenges emerged from Sweden and mainland Europe. The Czar's best artillery came from Tver—surpassing in quality the pieces of better-known Tula. Gorgeous, yet practical Samovars were also crafted here, as well as fine textiles and metalcraft of all types.

Tver was also the home of Afanasy Nikitin, who sailed to India well before the more heralded adventures of Spain's Vasco De Gama. Nikitin's journey was a fifteenth-century Odyssey during which he encountered challenges and perils of all types and managed to return to Russia with marvelous tales from the Orient. He is Russia's Christopher Columbus and his exploits are still much-read in Russia today. A marvelous monument to him stands on Tver's south Volga bank and a well-crafted beer from Tver bearing his name can now be found in Moscow pubs.[4]

In the mid-1700s, Tver caught the eye of the Czarina, Catherine II, thanks to its strategic location on the Volga, situated directly on the road between Moscow and St. Petersburg. She ordered that a palace be constructed in Tver so she could overnight on her coach ride between the two royal cities. Nicknamed the Putevoy Palace (The Travel Palace) by the locals, this 'modest' three-wing Palace captures the whimsy and wealth of the time.[5] Today, it houses art galleries.

Tver was an important regional center for riverine commerce in north-central Russia. In 1900, the first iron suspension bridge in Russia was built in Tver, modeled on the lovely Franz-Josef Bridge in Budapest. Before then, the north-south sides of Tver were connected by pontoon during warm months; winter ice made crossing untenable for a portion of each year.

Elena Kiryanova, in her lovely 1998 tome *Walks Along Old Tver*, writes of the pre-revolutionary city:

> *Tver was strikingly beautiful – lying on the banks of three rivers, sinking in green or covered in snow, pleasing with its embankments and open views. Steamships, barges, boats were all an inalienable part of the Volga landscape. The city's decorum was broken by markets with their lively sounds and hubbub. Carriages, cabs, passersby and their faces—all these provoke a non-false*

*interest of a man who is eager to understand the time
which passed and the city in that time—the city which
had stood up on the banks of the Volga in the deep
Middle Ages.*

By the late 1800s, Tver was a middle-sized Russian Industrial
Age city with a burgeoning proletariat, circumstances that made
it susceptible to the revolutionary currents of the late nineteenth
and early twentieth century. In 1905, an anti-Czarist revolt
erupted within the extraordinary laborers' tenements built by
industrialist and idealist Savva Morozov.[6] In 1917, Tver became
a Bolshevik stronghold during the Russian Revolution and
subsequent Civil War. The city was heavily industrialized during
the initial five-year plans of the early Soviet Union.

Renamed Kalinin in 1931 after President Mikhail Kalinin, the
ultimate Communist survivor during Stalin's brutal regime, the old
city lost whatever remaining luster it had when its old Orthodox
churches were shut down or destroyed. The craftsmanship which
had long distinguished the city was seconded to mass production
of textiles, chemicals, and railway cars. The numerous villages in
the area that specialized in potatoes, beets, cabbage, and rye were

all forcibly collectivized by 1933. Much of Kalinin's remaining intelligentsia was slaughtered during the 1936-38 Great Purge. In 1940, more than 4,000 Polish military officers were executed and buried in a field at Mednoye, a large village just twenty-five kilometers from the city center. (More on that later.)

Kalinin suffered heavily in World War II, but mercifully endured only two months of German occupation. Its Old Bridge was blown up by the retreating Red Army in October 1941, in the face of the onrushing Wehrmacht during Germany's ill-fated autumn drive to envelop Moscow. The Germans managed to cross the Volga by pontoon upstream of Kalinin, one of the few places where the German army breached the historic river during the war—a water barrier thousands of kilometers long that cuts through European Russia, past Stalingrad, to the Caspian Sea.[7]

Postwar Kalinin developed into a typical Soviet city, its crumbling historic core girdled by massive and poorly constructed apartment blocks built after the war. Its rich history and character were blotted out by the regime's indifference to pre-Revolutionary history—except when invoked to justify the current regime. Life in Kalinin devolved into tolerable mediocrity for most families, as long as one conformed to the rules. Quality goods were scarce, but there was enough of everything if one was willing to wait in the inevitable queues, and not bemoan the lack of choice.

Cracks in the Soviet edifice began to appear in the late 1970s and early 1980s. Most of the U.S.S.R.'s oil advantages had been squandered, and the flow of goods slowed to a trickle within many Soviet inner cities. The steady stream of casualties from the country's decade-long engagement in Afghanistan took its toll on the normally quiescent Soviet society and was especially visible in Kalinin, the site of one of the U.S.S.R.'s largest transport bases: Migelovo. Throughout the 1980s, the constant drone of transports coming from Afghanistan was inescapable for all Kalininites, especially the distinctive sound of the *Cherrniy Tulpen*—The Black Tulip. This aircraft's payload of death and sorrow consisted of Soviet-Afghan War dead being transported to Migelovo, a major processing point for the nation's war casualties, much like our Dover Air Force Base in Delaware.

An active anti-war chapter of Afghantsi (Afghan War veterans) took root in Kalinin and was not interfered with, thanks to Gorbachev's *glasnost*. A few veterans of the Afghan War took me to the graves of several of their comrades, where they left flowers. (Russians love flowers.) This was in the early 1990s, when Soviet society, though still relatively docile, was engaged in open dialogue about its future and dredging up the more difficult aspects of its past. Also evident in many people I talked to was a yearning to know more about the country's pre-Revolutionary, Czarist existence, beyond the propaganda fed to them since birth.

It was into this general environment that my group arrived by train in late June 1989. We stayed in the Hotel Volga, a reasonably well-built Soviet edifice with lousy plumbing, which stood a convenient five-minute walk from the university where we studied. The hotel was a major focal point in a city which had maybe eight places to eat out and even fewer to entertain. Its dining room was popular for large wedding parties and was important to both us and the Russians because it was one of the few places where one could negotiate for vodka and the hard-to-get, unlabeled local beer.

The U.S. dollar, which was illegal for Russians to own privately, was extremely coveted. The official dollar to ruble exchange rate was about 60 kopecks (100 kopecks to a ruble). The very active black market, however, traded between eight and ten rubles to the dollar—a rate which represented an almost 1,500 percent increase in the buying power of anyone trading dollars for rubles. Of course, rubles did not buy a lot of high-quality stuff at that time, but nonetheless, one could have plenty of all the basics, hire taxis, buy furs and travel at ridiculously low rates.

Because I was initially a somewhat paranoid U.S. Army officer, alone in the heart of the Soviet Union, I remained on good behavior, avoided the black market and carefully counted my expensive rubles. While my civilian fellow students lived regally, I lived like a pauper. As a result, I became somewhat of a joke to the local traders. Even so, oddly enough, years later, I became good friends with 'Alex,' one of the 'entrepreneurs' who would hang around our hotel looking to trade money and wares.

Directly opposite the hotel was our host school, Kalinin State University (KSU), which had a first-rate language department and a battery of dedicated teachers.[8] Our group must have been mildly frustrating for these teachers; they were used to a certain deference and respect which young American college students on summer break generally do not provide. Half of my group was extremely interested in improving their Russian and learning Russian culture, while the other half traded lots of money, partied and drank. All in all, a typical American college group.

We were exposed to a depth of authentic Russian culture I know few visitors received in Moscow and Leningrad. We studied the language, took field trips, learned some of Russia's beautiful native songs, were invited regularly into Russian homes and experienced multiple facets of Soviet society. The program director, a dynamic middle-aged woman named Tatiana, was truly progressive for the Soviet Union and tested the outer limits of *glasnost*. On the one hand, she invited Soviet businessmen to pitch trade ideas with us, while on the other, she exposed us to first-rate Marxist dialectics from several local 'sociologists.' It was quite something for me, in my bad Russian, to talk back and forth in front of sixty people, half of whom were Russians, about my perspective on the strengths and weaknesses of our respective systems. The fact that the Russians knew I was a U.S. Army officer—a former 'enemy' of the Soviet people—probably was one reason I was asked often to respond ... a role I accepted with cautious relish. This, of course, was still the era when it was inappropriate to speak poorly of Lenin, although just about anything else, especially Stalin, was fair game!

Kalinin's university—like all Russian scholastic endeavors—was a very serious place. After seeing the emphasis the Russians put on education, it is more understandable to me how they put men into space, built the extraordinary Moscow metro and maintained such excellence in the fine arts, all within a society which fundamentally eschewed individualism and culture.

It is not easy to be accepted into a Russian university. We quietly marveled at the earnest looks of the young candidate students as they waited patiently in line with their entire families—all dressed in their Sunday best—to take weekend entrance exams. To pass and be accepted into a university program presaged a gateway into academia that in the old U.S.S.R. meant the possibility of a better, more mobile life. Academicians enjoyed status and were decently paid and housed. The alternative was a lifetime of more menial work with very little possibility to enhance one's lifestyle. Entrepreneurs officially did not exist.

Each of us in the group had a personal escort. Mine was a young eighteen-year-old lad named Alexei who had hair reaching his belt and loved rock-and-roll. A real live young MTVer, but with no MTV to watch! He wore the same blue jeans and blue work shirt every day. He was a sweet, downy-faced kid but was cloyingly around all the time—to this day I don't know what his role was—though he really did try to bond with me. Some of the senior class organizers were clearly young *Komsomol* (youth organization of the Communist Party) and therefore had a control and reporting function. But it was obvious that only a few believed in its claptrap anymore. Almost all of our escorts provided their first American visitors with unbelievable hospitality and unfettered access to Kalinin. As the summer progressed I gravitated away from most of them and managed to meet numerous other Kalininites from different, non-University walks of life.

That first summer in Kalinin supplied me with many images and personalities I shall never forget. Particularly memorable was a near-daily routine to walk across the city to the banks of the Volga, where we spent lazy afternoons playing chess on the banks until well into the evening, our game illuminated by June's long 'white nights.' We often waded into the muddy Volga to swim across to the other bank, while dodging barges and the river patrol. On most days I was treated to the spectacle of numerous Soviet military aircraft—IL-76s', AN-20s and AN-22s, including no doubt the dreaded Black Tulip—flying low directly over us on final approach to Migelovo airbase. The sky over Tver was rarely quiet.

This was still only 1989, two years before U.S. military aircraft began visiting Soviet airbases during Operation Provide Hope, a U.S. Air Force program to provide humanitarian aid to former Soviet republics. It was a heady feeling, always tinged with sober caution, to see the Soviet military up close and observe the huge turboprops and jets. It was especially exhilarating for a young tactical (combat) intelligence officer like me, who over the years had laboriously studied all forms of Soviet combat equipment from afar. Some Soviet students who knew I was a U.S. Army officer actually invited me to pick ripe berries within the air base's fence line—something they said they did regularly. Although I was tempted, I decided not to push my luck and declined the probably sincere offer.

My first return visit to Kalinin was in June 1990. Although the city looked exactly the same, the atmosphere was different. Gorbachev's reform express was still in full swing and people were much less tentative than even the year before about what they said about the old regime. Even that most hallowed of icons, Lenin, was open to pot-shots.

I arrived on Tver's birthday—celebrated the third Sunday of every June—to the sight of a large block party along the 500-meter long walking mall named Tverskaya Street. The distinctive tinny sound of Czarist era bells was ringing everywhere and many stands that were selling various goods openly displayed the old city's Imperial coat of arms. Especially surprising was the sight of a number of men strutting around in Czarist and Cossack uniforms. The city was still in the U.S.S.R., after all. A few days later, July 1, 1990, Kalinin's original name—Tver—was officially restored.

At dusk, which is more like twilight and doesn't set in until 10:00 p.m. in summer, the entire city (it seemed to me) turned out along both banks of the Volga to watch the best fireworks display the city could muster. Here, and again in 1995, I was struck by the relative innocence and lack of cynicism, the sheer joy, and awe at the display. Little girls in bows and ribbons and little boys in shorts were held closely by their parents, as they all oohed and aahed at the fireworks igniting above the river. It was a modest display by New York City standards, but one greatly appreciated by the hard-working or laid-off local population who now had fewer meaningful public diversions than during the Soviet era. At show's end, the crowd dispersed, faced with the prospect of a dreary week of work ahead and being herded on Monday morning onto the city's badly overcrowded and maintained trams and trolley buses.

I recall thinking then, in 1990, how naive many of these Russians seemed in their yearning and nostalgia toward all the Imperial paraphernalia. Then again, an idealized, romantic view of Czarist times was for many Russians the only frame of reference they had to compare with the communist era. The concept of a benevolent Czar and/or democracy and a restructured economy were psychological placebos which underpinned economic and societal change.

My visit took place during the heart of Gorbachev's short-lived prohibition against excessive vodka consumption—a prohibition that came close to derailing all that he had achieved in opening Soviet society. Adding insult to injury was the fact that the U.S.S.R. was simultaneously going through a massive 'nicotine fit', thanks to an acute shortage of both domestic and imported cigarettes. It was as if the U.S.S.R.'s body politic was experiencing massive congestive heart failure when deprived of the things that helped typical Russians cope with stress and increasingly difficult times.

Lines, of course, were longest outside places that sold tobacco. As a foreigner, I could pay for services with cigarettes. When I finally gave up trying to pay for everything only with rubles, I often would hail a taxi—really just a moonlighting car—by holding out a pack of Marlboros, which was the most-coveted brand.

In Tver, the crafty always knew where to find illegal alcohol. One location was the central taxi stand, where cabbies sold the contraband right out of their trunks. There you could always find that late-night bottle of vodka…at a premium, of course. The contraband cost about 30 rubles, whereas in a store, if available, the same bottle was only five to ten rubles. The ruble had been re-pegged that year from 60 kopecks to about six rubles to the dollar, so one can quickly see that the traders were getting $5 to $6 per bottle on the black market, in a country where an average worker's buying power had fallen to about $60 per month.

Alcohol wasn't the only item that cost a small fortune on the black market. A pack of Marlboros cost about 15 rubles, or $3. Levi 501s cost 600 rubles ($100) and a good pair of Nikes or Reeboks between 500-1,000 rubles ($80-$160). One cab driver wryly remarked to me that he could buy a nice used Zhiguli car for five pairs of new Nikes or ten blue jean jackets. The speculation in vodka got so rife that during my last night in Tver, the local police went on a citywide roundup of taxis and cars shuttling illegal vodka. I'll never forget hearing my very street-wise friend Igor chuckling about the raid with his friends as we enjoyed our bottle of vodka. Just a couple of hours later, the local news reported that the GAU (local traffic police) had confiscated 1,850 bottles of liquor from traders unfortunate enough to be caught.

The period 1990-1991 was the best time to have hard currency in Russia. The prices favoring foreigners were incredibly skewed while the central state bank clumsily tried to keep up with the more agile hard currency market.

In December 1991, I returned to Tver yet again. I arrived to find a different Russia, one I had never seen before: a dark, depressing winter in a typical Russian city. The mere seven hours of daylight contrasted vividly with the eighteen hours of daylight/twilight in summertime. In the far distance, the clouds reflected an eerie firelight hue. When I got closer I saw that the city had lit the top of its ten-story high monument to its WWII fallen, annually commemorated on December 16. This year was the fiftieth anniversary of Tver's liberation from its two-month occupation by German forces during World War II.

On this trip, Igor introduced me to his friends in the trucking business who, in those early days of the new Russia, lived in a frozen compound guarded by attack dogs. At that time, having access to food commodities, plus the means to distribute them, gave aggressive entrepreneurs power and influence. Igor's friends were particularly proud of the large shipment of Jaffa orange juice they had recently scored from Israel. Their coup was just after a period when bananas were still considered exotica.

As the 1990s marched on in Tver, one saw more and more 'New Russians', a label that parodied Lenin's 'New Soviet Man' ideal, and now served as a sarcastic pejorative to describe Russia's growing nouveau riche. There is no traditional 'old money' in Russia today, only fortunes amassed mostly by slicksters and opportunistic former U.S.S.R. Communist Party members. These creatures, prevalent in any radically changing economic environment where initiative and the strong arm outpace the law, were indicative of all that was right and wrong about economic reform in Russia. The typical New Russian turned his back on the rest of Russian society and the law to get ahead. Reviled by most Russians who have not prospered, these nouveau riche often sport designer clothes of execrable taste, and roar imperiously around Russian cities in late model Western cars and jeeps. Some strut, swagger and simply hang out around their cars in the middle of the day, thereby earning the enmity of many older Russians who are out of work or employed at marginal wages and trying to stay above subsistence living.

Other young Russians, mostly entrepreneurs who have learned to work the system, have graduated to a new level of sophistication. They dress better, are more understated, have children and are building a new aristocracy that parallels and over time will supersede the old opportunistic Communists and gangster class. They are the new *nomenklatura*, and they share with a nascent middle class of shopkeepers and business managers a vested interest in ensuring that Russia does not swing back to Central Control.

As loathsome and *ne kulturni* as many of the New Russians are, one cannot forget that they played a major role in the Russian reform process and now act as a major barrier to conservative revanchism in Russia.

Organized crime in the U.S.S.R. was the first group to take advantage of relaxed Soviet laws to stock kiosks with high-quality goods and infuse Russian society with some sense of private enterprise. After Intourist and the Party apparatus, organized crime was the only independent element within Russia that possessed the infrastructure and the ruthlessness to get goods to market. The fact that the resulting economic 'liberalization' came replete with gangsters, protection rackets and the wholesale corruption of the legal and law enforcement system is inescapable, but they, not the corporations and ministries, are to be credited with planting the first tangible economic seeds among the Russian population.

The good news is that the go-go early 1990s, when 'get rich quick' was the norm and prostitutes comprised part of the aristocracy, seem to be slowly and inexorably giving way to more credible businesses and institutions as the laws slowly catch up to the criminals. The conundrum Russian society continues to face today is the necessity of rooting out the more violent, ill-disciplined and blatant criminals, while quietly institutionalizing those who have become 'part of the system.'

This approach is not without precedent. Our own Gilded Age robber barons—Rockefeller, Carnegie, Vanderbilt, and others— grew in time to be part of our respectable American business and social elite. Complicating this process in Russia, however, are the kleptocratic tendencies of the many people working in the Russian government, ministries, and banks who are reluctant to pay taxes and instead stash their hard currency, such as International Monetary Fund dollars, abroad.

Economically, Tver is a microcosm of Moscow and St. Petersburg. From 1989 to 1999, I watched the careers of young black marketers and entrepreneurs evolve from relatively small-time, two-bit status to running serious businesses, awash in dollars. I know one young man in Tver who in 1989 was trading money and goods, by 1990 had one truck and by 1991 had a fleet of seven trucks which serviced all of the city's ice cream kiosks. (After vodka and cigarettes, ice cream kiosks were the next most profitable business, in the era before a massive influx of videotapes and electronics kiosks). Today he owns a large import-export company in a nicely renovated building on the edge of town. He still keeps a shotgun by his desk and a large Doberman on the premises. He proudly showed me thousands of dollars which he keeps in a large state-of-the-art safe because he, for good reason, doesn't trust the banking system. I suspect he pays minimal taxes.

ALEX

ONE OF THE MOST COLORFUL characters I met in Tver was Alexei, nicknamed Alex. Alex was Tver's main young black marketeer in 1989 who, with his friend Sasha, would hang around the entrance of the Hotel Volga. He wore a bright blue New York Giants jersey, no doubt traded off the back of an earlier tourist. Alex was a charismatic, stocky and blond twenty-five-year-old who spoke decent English and quickly befriended my class. At the time this really irritated me because I saw exactly what he was doing. He inevitably became our student group's main currency trader—as well as throughput for a lot of our clothing and tradable items—which was precisely his objective. Though currency trading was forbidden by Soviet law, neither the bulk of my class nor Alex felt any risk. My relations with Alex were quite frosty initially.

He quickly learned that I was a somewhat uptight military guy, wouldn't trade money, and openly disapproved of his actions. Over time, and as I loosened up, we developed a humorous *modus vivendi* and bantered back and forth as I came in and out of the hotel.

When I came back to Kalinin the second time, in June 1990, I was forced to stay at the mosquito-ridden Motel Tver, which sat astride the main highway between Moscow and Leningrad on the edge of town. All foreign travelers visiting Tver had to stay at the state-controlled Intourist motel unless *Derjjey* received an official invitation or were in a special program such as my University group. This requirement, couched in terms of safety and hygienic reasons, was an obvious control measure to keep track of and watch over foreigners.

After checking in, I walked past a new kiosk in the hotel and there was Alex with a very attractive college-age lady.

The scenario was certainly innovative. When I first came to Tver, the only place in town to pick up any Western goods or quality Russian handicrafts was the hard currency *Beriozka* (the birch tree) Shop, which stood in the center of Tver on Soviet Street. One could buy goods there only for Western currency –

rubles were not accepted. Actually, Russian Citizens could go in there if they had dollars or other western currency. Until about 1991, every good-sized Russian city and foreigner-focused hotel in the Intourist chain had a *Beriozka* Shop, which was closed to ordinary Russian citizens. We as foreigners could always dip into the *Beriozka* Shop—there was never a queue—to pick up a cold soda, occasionally a cold beer and some Western snacks and candy. As the summer progressed, my sensitivity to life in the provincial U.S.S.R. increased, and I began to feel guilty when leaving the shop carrying one of their colorful shopping bags. I could see mostly resigned, yet curiously not resentful looks on the faces of locals eyeing us coming out of the store.

Alex had somehow arranged with the Tver Motel to set up his own kiosk to replace the fading *Beriozka* Shop there. It was stocked full of Russian handicrafts and Soviet military items, which were fast becoming the collector's rage for foreigners traveling through the U.S.S.R. Having a privately owned kiosk in an Intourist hotel in those days surely meant cash arrangements with the hotel itself, the fledgling local mafia, and the on-site security types.

Alex staffed the kiosk with pretty girls and ran it as a twenty-four-hour-a-day operation. The kiosk girl slept on a cot behind the counter when there were no customers; the site was secure because it sat in the Motel's lobby. I would often see Alex when I came back to the motel, no matter the hour, and he would tell me a lot about how business and life were evolving in Tver.

His story is worth telling. Until 1994, Alex lived a charmed life. He ran several kiosks in Tver and was branching out into other businesses he did not tell me about. He owned fast cars and would drive every summer to the Black Sea. Cocky and flush with money, he eventually tripped himself up by investing in MMM.

MMM was a pyramid type voucher scheme based on individuals like Alex buying shares of privatizing companies and then bringing in more investors. The scheme briefly flourished before collapsing completely in 1994, destroying the savings of most who had invested. Millions of people across Russia were affected. Alex was wiped out. It hurt both banks and individuals and put a squealing stop to much of the get-rich-quick mentality that permeated Russia at the time. It also badly hurt many small investors—the second big blow of three in the 1990s (two currency devaluations and MMM)[9].

Alex then hit a string of more bad luck that ended in his full bankruptcy, loss of his car and apartment. He had to hide from numerous debtors, some of whom threatened dire consequences if not paid. In the middle of his personal nadir, we met in the summer of 1995, sat down in the city park with a sack of the excellent Afanasy Tver-produced beers and talked. We became light-headed and garrulous as we drank four jumbo bottles each of the well-made, dark beer under the hot summer sun. Having just climbed out of his lowest trough—a period which included brief contemplation of suicide—Alex needed to talk. He told me his whole story, especially about his so-called rise and fall in Tver's local business community.

The following year, Alex's life took a turn for the better. He hooked up with some of my closest Tver friends who were living in Moscow and running an Italian-linked high-tech fiber-optic subsidiary for Siemens. He is now (1999) their sales representative in Tver and has shed most of his high-speed, carefree, entrepreneurial habits. Alex has become a very strong salesperson, although I fear some of the spirit has been knocked out of him. A drinker, he recently lost his driver's license during a tough Russian anti-drinking and driving campaign and uses a forged license to get around.

In contrast, Alex's best friend and 1989 black-marketing accomplice, Sasha, managed to leave Russia about seven years ago and is now the vice president of an Internet service provider in Seattle.

In July 1995, on the heels of a unique trip to the three Buddhist Republics of Russia (Kalmykia, Buryatia, and Tuva), I returned once again to Tver. I grabbed a cab outside the train station, haggled a bit on the fare and rode off to the old Volga Hotel, where I had started staying in 1993 on my visits to the city. (Goodbye, Motel Tver!) I immediately tracked down my old friend Igor, who was working as a caretaker for a Karate Club in Tver's old Proletarka workers district, near the Volga riverfront in the center of town. More than most Russians, Igor has ridden the stormy swells of *glasnost* and *perestroika*, with alternating successes and failures.

I'll let my diary take over from here:

Walking through old czarist industrial dormitories, one sees a different urban Russia—broken roads, people eking out a slightly more than subsistence existence— Zyuganov, Zhirinovsky country. Water pumps in the street, family pushing milk carts—red brick industry next to white Stalinesque high-rises sitting among a jumble of multi-hued wooden houses, cottages really, with the hum of broken down elektreechkas in the distance. I frankly don't know how people lived during the Communist regime. Judging from the dwellings today not much better (or worse) ... however ... their buying power, pensions etcetera were in balance with the economy, whatever goods which were available were affordable—hence the almost fond nostalgia towards the 'good old days'. Expectations led only to higher prices and for many a perfectly useless concept like democracy and freedom of speech.

The Proletarka District of Tver where Igor worked is worth briefly expounding upon. Built by Savva Morozov, a Russian industrialist and idealist (1862-1905), this massive red brick, turn-of-the-twentieth-century factory complex still stands despite almost no renovation in one hundred years. The impressive complex, replete with well-built workers dormitories, stands as mute testimony to Morozov's skills, energy and unusual concern for the Industrial Age working class. One huge building, known as the Paris Barracks, due to its French Art Nouveau style, still houses labor within its vast dormitory for an aging textile factory nearby. Nowadays, however, whole families (including an Air Force Lieutenant-Colonel I encountered) live in the building's small overcrowded rooms. Morozov's fate remains murky. Some say he took his own life when the dark nature of the Marxism he supported revealed itself under Lenin. Others say he was murdered.[10]

My visits to see Igor at the Proletarka gym were never without incident. Invariably I met a parade of unusual characters, far different from the more refined and well-behaved University crowd. Each arrival would usually begin with a quick stop-by at the local kiosk servicing Proletarka with alcohol and snacks— always my treat because everything was so cheap for my dollar. After recovering from the initial shock of seeing an American in such a depressed district, the three young ladies working inside the kiosk were always amused by my visits and purchases.

The gym complex Igor worked in was the former Communist Party Headquarters and Meeting Hall in Proletarka. Within its red brick walls, many speeches had been given and many medals awarded to the industrial shock troops of the district's proletariat, who together supported a textile and railway car factory. The owner of the gym's Karate Club was a tough and very racist former Spetsnaz—Special Forces—soldier. He and his crowd would have made an interesting paleolithic sociological study.

Many of my mid-1990s evenings in Tver were spent in the cramped confines of the gym's office suite where we all watched movies and argued about life in Russia. Despite the roughness of the gym crowd they were mesmerized by the film rendition of Mikhail Bulgakov's *Heart of a Dog*, film-noir about the transplant of a drunkard's pituitary gland and testicles into a dog to parody the New Soviet Man. Even with my sketchy knowledge of Russian, I found the film marvelous. It surely would have landed its director in jail during the Soviet era! [11]

In another amusing and insightful moment, we were arguing politics one night during the run-up to the second 1996 run-off election. The gym owner, a staunch proponent of Communist Party standard-bearer Gennady Zyuganov, was arguing vociferously that democracy will never work in Russia and that the old Brezhnev days were better. During the argument, a sexually explicit scene popped up on the television and caught the old Communist's attention. Igor, moving in for the kill, flicked off the TV every time his opponent's eyes strayed to the screen, a teasing gesture that set off a row. Throughout, Igor pressed, "This is Communist censorship, do you like it?" to the frustrated older man, after which we poured some more vodka and continued our discussion as if nothing had happened.

One evening in the gym's office I met another unique fellow, a former Northern Fleet sailor named Ruslan. A short, swarthy Daghestani, Ruslan rather fancied himself a ladies' man and, like many alpha males, talked incessantly about his numerous conquests. This lad was no Islamic fundamentalist!

In 1989, he docked at the huge Norfolk Naval Base in Virginia as a crew-member of the Soviet missile cruiser *Marshal Ustinov*. The occasion was one of the very first U.S. port visits by the Soviet Navy during the thawing Cold War. Ruslan was amazed by the spacious crew quarters and cleanliness of the U.S. ships, as well as the goods each U.S. sailor owned. Living up to type, he got drunk with some U.S. sailors while on off-ship liberty—the language chasm didn't matter—and was detained by the shore patrol for disorderly behavior. The whole group of American and Russian sailors was then dressed down by a U.S. Admiral who happened to be passing by. One of the tipsy Soviet sailors, already sporting a U.S. Navy hat, gave the Admiral a crisp, All-American salute. Ruslan was convinced he spied the shadow of a smile cross the senior officer's face.

While in port, the Soviet ship's mess served rotten potatoes to the crew. One gnarly spud was hurled at a passing U.S. helicopter. Thirty minutes later, the helicopter returned and dumped a bushel of fresh potatoes on the *Ustinov*'s deck—a surprise special delivery that created quite a stir on board.

Far from shy, Ruslan shared with us his fantasy of having vodka, caviar, and dumplings in New York's finest restaurant while surrounded by a dozen prostitutes. In the next breath, he swore that he had had sex with a prostitute on the pedestal of Tver's Lenin statue, which, if true, was playing with red-hot fire in the old U.S.S.R. In retrospect, Ruslan could simply have been spinning lascivious sailor's yarns about his exploits for our entertainment. Even so, if they were nothing more than figments of his imagination, they still warrant publishing for their sheer brashness and creativity.

BANKING

"A Ruble in the Hand is Worth Two in the Bank"

(Current Russian Wisdom)

IN 1989, ONLY FOREIGNERS AND Russians operating State-owned hard currency businesses could convert dollars to rubles in State Banks at the official rate. Pensioners could still, with some confidence, deposit their ruble savings. By 1991-1992, the situation had changed. By then, the bulk of most pensioners' lifetime savings had been wiped out by the ruble's hyperinflation and official devaluation in January 1991. Independent banks, usually financed with illegally begot money, began appearing throughout Tver. The new banks offered high interest rates and provided terrifying uncertainty for desperate people looking for somewhere to deposit their evaporating wages and pensions. Many of these so-called banks were, simply put, confidence operations, which opened and closed within months or a year, the owners disappearing mysteriously into the proverbial night.

The main branch of the Tver Universal bank is a blatant example of this financial hubris. From 1995 to 1996, a huge (for Tver) $20 million, modern glass-walled edifice was built in the heart of Tver. It looked grotesquely out of place amid the decaying traditional or dreary Soviet architecture surrounding it. When I arrived in Tver in October 1997, the building sat there unopened. Even now, in 1999, its hulk is rusting and still unoccupied. Apparently, the local bankers who built it had links to the Communist Party—not surprising in industrial Tver, which tends toward a Communist plurality during elections.

After Boris Yeltsin won the 1996 presidential election, locals say that the Russian Central Bank strangled Tver Universal to near bankruptcy by limiting loans and incentives, forcing it to shut down the new branch. Of course, it didn't help Tver locals that the Tver Universal had already poured millions of their deposits into constructing this colossal white elephant. No small wonder people are so jaded and have so little confidence in the banking system.

One friend, who works as an attorney for another branch of Tver Universal, confesses his fears getting mixed up with the wrong types associated with the bank. After all, many of Russia's rich are criminals. He earns a good salary for Tver ($500 a month) and keeps a low profile. Before the August 1998 financial collapse, he bought an apartment in Tver for the princely sum of $13,500. He was able to secure a five-year loan at fifteen percent interest, adjustable with inflation. Because he works in the bank and has a wife and child living in Tver, he was able to secure this preferred loan. For a higher credit risk, with little to no collateral, the bank charges approximately one hundred eighty percent over five years—meaning a $13,000 loan would pay in at about $23,000. Because only people with high cash flow would risk borrowing at that rate, the bank can get away with making usurious loans and uses its 'collection agency' as insurance.

Although the situation is slowly improving, the hunt for credible and affordable insurance in Tver is just about impossible for the typical Russian. A dented car remains dented, its owner having little recourse. Getting a loan today in Russia is serious business; falling behind or reneging can bring dire consequences on the typical borrower. Simply put, no serious bank is without several 'notches' to its credit, a notch meaning serious harm to a creditor attempting to skip his loan. Few militiamen have the desire or the inclination—especially given their abysmal salaries—to track down deadbeats; hence this type of harshly meted out justice is handled by privately hired 'bill collectors.' The collectors are the only guarantee a bank has that its loans will be paid on time. Incomprehensible to us, it makes eminent sense in a country where the laws of the jungle will rule the marketplace until enforceable laws pull even with the criminals. No wonder so many foreign investors steer clear of the exasperating Russian business scene.

Another Russian friend, Larisa, formerly a philology student at KSU (English, German), recounted her husband's business trials and travails, an Indian citizen whom she met at the Tver Medical Institute. After achieving his doctorate, as many foreigners do at the Institute, he decided to remain in Tver and opened several small businesses, including a small bar near the city center. The bar initially was successful. It filled a void for increasingly upscale Tverites. Like every small business in Russia, the place was protected by representatives of the local Mafia (*kreesha*—the 'wing'), which varied their fees according to the business condition of the enterprise. After all, it is not a good thing to kill the fatted calf with excessively high fees. Their two collectors became a near everyday presence and were accepted as part of the bar's scenery. One day, the pair didn't show up and later were found dead in a burnt-out car on the edge of town. Shortly afterward, the young Indian bar proprietor was ambushed by gangsters who jumped him in a dark apartment building stairwell on his way home from work. They put a gun to his head and forced his wife to open the apartment door. While the couple's baby screamed in its crib, the four masked thieves taped their mouths shut, tied them up, and rifled through the apartment stealing approximately $1,000 cash and their TV, VCR, and videos.

The militia, in this case, responded quickly, perhaps because they were not part of the local 'take'. Within two weeks, the four bandits, including an ethnic Volga German, were arrested. The case revealed that the crooks were not organized crime, but simply petty hoods who had followed the owner home from the bar cased the apartment and set the trap.

This was easy to do. Almost every Russian apartment building is still public property and is open to the street. Most are miserably maintained; only an elite few are equipped with an entry control system. The entryways are wide-open and often reek like urinals. The stairs and elevators are dark or dimly lit, and anyone can lurk on them for a prospective target. Therefore, the moment most Russians leave their apartments—relative oases compared to the darkness and filth outside their door—they must be alert. In the West, one finds this phenomenon only in the worst public housing projects and tenements. It's virtually everywhere in Russia, which is a depressing way to enter the world every day.

On the other hand, the much-reported criminal danger to tourists in Russia is exaggerated by our media. It is true that Russians are still killing each other at an unprecedented rate, however, it is rare that the typical tourist is a victim of violent crime. The bulk of the shootings are gangland in nature, as competing mafias stake and re-stake their ground. Petty crime is the typical tourist's biggest threat, but the danger is no worse than in New York, London or Paris. In Tver, or Russia at large, I've never been accosted except by roving packs of Gypsies.

The incident which jangled me most in Tver took place in summer 1990 when I was walking through the city park and two young men asked if I wanted to buy some hashish. In the States, this would not have fazed me, but in the U.S.S.R. it did because I feared being set up. If the men were selling hash—which in this instance was highly probable, but still unusual—it showed me firsthand yet another example of Soviet internal controls breaking down and that people were losing respect for law enforcement.

Politics & History

An aide goes to Boris Yeltsin:

> Aide: *"Boris Nicholaevitch, I have good news and bad news."*
>
> Yeltsin: *"Give me the bad news first."*
>
> Aide: *"Zyuganov won sixty percent of the vote."*
>
> Yeltsin: *"And the good news?"*
>
> Aide: *"You received sixty-six percent!"*

In June 1996, I returned to Tver for over a week. With the all-important national elections looming, I sensed this was a critical moment for Russia's current and future history, and I wanted to be there during most of the unfolding drama.

In the United States and the West, much airtime was devoted to four subjects: the return of the Communists under

Gennady Zyuganov,[12] the radical Zhirinovsky factor,[13] General Lebed,[14] and President Boris Yeltsin's health.[15] The most common lines of thinking reported by Moscow-based Western press included: 1) all the older Russians will vote for the communists or nationalists; 2) Yeltsin is finished, and 3) that the terrible crime rate would move Russia toward Lebed. All proved to be cliched and ultimately wrong. Out in Tver, my private canvassing revealed that the issue was far more complex.

On election morning, I took the early commuter train from Moscow to Tver. I wanted to see the election in the provinces rather than in the capital. This train, affectionately nicknamed the *elektreechka*, is a great way to see 'the real Russia.' Filthy, overcrowded, but dirt cheap, these commuter trains depart regularly from every decent-sized Russian city and radiate out in every direction into the hinterland, up to two hundred kilometers. In the past, when nonstandard goods and foodstuffs were hard to come by, the trains were full every morning with droves of people, mostly women, children, and older men, carrying an assortment of sacks, bags, and carts to buy from the better-stocked city markets. At day's end, tired, they returned to home by the *elektreechka*, sitting on wood or wicker seats, or even standing for several hours, with their day's haul.

Few foreigners and no tourists travel on these trains (most ride the elite Red Arrow or Aurora), but riding the rails on these decrepit, Latvian-built, electric trains is a true prism for observing authentic Russian life. Numerous times I have struck up conversations with inquisitive fellow passengers from the heartland who never see foreigners. They're frank and untainted by the inner-city cosmopolitanism of Moscow or St. Petersburg. In my brief election canvassing, most were voting for Yeltsin, including one ancient veteran of Stalingrad who stated he was voting for his grandchildren's future. To me, this was remarkable and indicative of the incredible patience of the Russians. This older man knew that his sons and daughters would continue to have tough lives. Still, even in the face of his diminished pension, prestige, and quality of life, he recognized that Russia absolutely had to go forward with the reform process. He was not going to be part of that process, but maybe his grandchildren would ultimately benefit.

Upon arriving at Tver, I went looking for my friend Igor, who lived in a deteriorating wood house with his mother in Tver's residential old quarter near the Church of White Trinity. Czarist-era houses were surrounding the church built in the old Russian log cabin style—colorful, all wood, and no more than two to three stories high.

The Church of White Trinity was the only church permitted to hold Russian Orthodox services during the Soviet era.[16] I visited one service in 1989 and was struck by the length and solemnity of the ceremony. It appeared that a group of very old *babushkas*, many of whom had probably lost their menfolk in the war or from bad health, were keeping the religious flame alive. They were successful. During the last seven years, Tver has seen a vibrant proliferation of Orthodox churches, both rebuilt and brand-new.

Igor was nowhere to be found. His neighbors, Sasha, Alexi, Luba, and Nina, found me wandering around and invited me inside their simple home—an example of typical Russian hospitality. I noticed that both bedrooms were centered on a large color television and video recorder. For many Russians, a

TV/VCR is the most prestigious and used item on a household's status list.

The two men wanted to drink, and the women tried to slow them down—a common scenario in most Slavic countries. Both Alexander and Alexi, aged well beyond their years, were workers in the local Tver railway car factory. Their salary was about 500,000 rubles a month, around $100. ($1.00 = approximately 5,000R in 1996). After two months of no wages, the state-run factory finally paid them—a well-timed gesture considering the election the next day.

Luba and Nina worked in the local textile factory and received about $60 a month. As our conversation developed—fueled by ever-present vodka and a badly narrated Claude Van Damme movie in the background—we inevitably turned to politics. I was surprised to learn that of the four, two would vote for General Lebed (Order!) and two for the liberal reformer Yavlinsky (Future!).

Being taken by surprise was a recurring problem for me. Even with my assorted Russian experiences, I was full of pre-conceived notions concerning the country's electorate. For example, I was sure that these four persons would vote for the Communists or nationalists. But I was dead wrong. For me, the chief revelation was how many of the older, more traditional Russians, workers, pensioners, and those not benefiting in the current regime did not vote for Zyuganov or Zhirinovsky and instead voted for the other candidates. Another cliché fell: all these people—lumped together by stereotype—would vote for the Communists. They remembered!

As always, Igor's neighbors peppered me with questions: "How do you live in the U.S.A.? Do we live better than the Russians? How much do you make in salary?" Although I rarely duck candor, I did not tell them that I earn several thousand dollars a month and own two cars—inconceivable to most Russians. I've found that when talking to the less fortunate in Russian society, it is always better to downplay our incredible American standard of living so as not to build resentment and envy.

While Western press anticipated gloom and doom throughout Russia, Election Day 1996 in Tver was overwhelmingly ordinary and uneventful. Nowhere were there modern-day Spartacists and Fascists duking it out in the streets.

Many people went to *dachas* in the country to enjoy the pretty summer weather. Polling booths were set up in schools and public buildings, similar to what we do in the U.S. There was no sign of excessive security, and I did not have a problem entering the local polling precinct with my good friend Ivan, who got a head-nod from the precinct manager to allow me inside.

The voting sheet had a list of fourteen candidates covering the full spectrum of the Russian political landscape. I was allowed to study it and even took several pictures inside. This simply would not have been possible during the Soviet regime.

Ivan's wife voted for Yeltsin, while Ivan, an unabashed monarchist and disenchanted by the entire field, voted *proteev vsehh*—against all candidates. We then strolled through the neighborhood and saw a small gaggle of people striding by with a red ballot box in hand. In Tver, local electoral officials carry the ballots to the old and infirm. In this case, the ballot box was carried by one of the local Communist Party officials who was, in turn, cheerfully escorted by several people from other political parties to prevent any electoral shenanigans.

Late election night, over vodka shots in the sitting room of the

Proletarka gym where he worked, Igor, a former Georgian sailor (who was still amazed to have seen a U.S. frigate in Vladivostok sometime earlier), and I watched the election returns come in on television, much as one would have watched Walter Cronkite or David Brokaw in the U.S. Returns first came in from the Far East and Siberia, where economic and social disenchantment with the regime were particularly high—they were reputedly Zyuganov and Zhirinovsky country. We were surprised early on by Yeltsin's and Lebed's relative strength to Zyuganov's small majority in areas where he had to win big. In five years, Mikhail Gorbachev received a paltry one to two percent of the vote, indicative of how much Russia had changed in five years. I believe that in time Gorbachev will be looked at as one of the great men of the twentieth century—even by post-2000 AD generations of Russians.[17]

We really don't give the Russian people much credit for independent thinking. Hardened by continued adversity, they have become quite wise as a thinking polity, in contrast to their reputation as sheep always looking for a strong figure to lead them. If ever there was an opportunity to turn the clock back, the Russians had it on June 16 and July 3, 1996. They chose not to. In the end, Yeltsin, the quasi-democrat was re-elected.

Two years later, August 17, 1998, the nation faced an economic catastrophe that would have brought down most governments down in the West and surely would have inspired angry citizens to take to the streets. Emergency measures taken by the government devalued the ruble and wiped out savings accounts and more overnight. The Russian population did not riot in the face of such general social and economic malaise is a testament to the grim lessons the Russians had learned under the old regime. My friend Vadim observed: "August 17 was bad, very bad, but we have seen much worse in Russia."

To understand today's seemingly schizophrenic Russians, one must study their tortured twentieth-century history. Consider the immense agony of a population which, within thirty years (WWI 1914-1918; Russian Civil War 1917-1921; famine 1919-1921; collectivization and man-made famine 1930-1933: The Great Purge 1936-1938 and WWII 1941-1945), lost more than forty million people, of which probably half were civilian innocents or noncombatants. The deaths were most often from unnatural, often brutal causes.

Arguably, no large population on earth has suffered the way the Russians have in the twentieth century. One cannot even begin to compare our own national calamities with the Russians—the differences in scale are mind-boggling.

Four seminal events stand out among numerous grim examples. First, the Russian Revolution a century ago yanked Russia out of civilized Europe, the consequences of which left the country under mind-numbing totalitarian rule for seventy years. Our American Civil War was bloody, with great battles and plenty of national suffering, but pales in comparison to the bloodshed, atrocities, and dislocation of the 1917-1921 Russian Revolution. Our Civil War helped reinforce our nation, confirm it, while the Russian Revolution violently and completely destroyed one system, only to build something utterly malevolent in its place. Millions of Russians died during this bloody period. Whatever little culture survived within the old regime was ruthlessly snuffed out or exported during the White Russian Diaspora, when millions of Russians fled the country to escape the new Bolshevik regime.

In the U.S., our major economic calamity was the Great Depression in the 1930s, a period when many people suffered; some died, but few starved to death. In contrast, between five million and seven million Soviets perished in two terrible famines—1919-1921 and 1930-1933, the second one man-made.[18]

In the United States, the closest thing we have ever had to a politically-driven purge was the troubling McCarthy witch hunt in the mid-1950s, during which several thousand Americans were slandered, some lost their jobs, but only a few died—by suicide, stress, or heartbreak. In contrast, The Great Terror (or Great Purge) from 1936-38 touched every Soviet family, and no corner of the country escaped it. Numerous millions—most of them average, normal citizens—were executed, and other millions were deported on nebulous grounds for 'conspiracies' against the state. Entire ethnic nations were summarily relocated; an entire generation of orphaned children grew up as wards of the state.

The Terror was the 'other' great crime of the twentieth century.

Hundreds of books have been written about the Holocaust of World War II, but only a few exist on the Terror. Yet the Russian psyche was scarred deeply by an event so horrendous and so palpably evil that it is unfathomable to me that it remains just a paragraph in most of our history books.[19]

Finally, there was 'The War'. The United States paid a grief-filled butcher's bill in blood and lives during World War II, but many of us have no knowledge or comprehension of the absolute horrors which befell the Soviet people from 1941-1945. Quite simply, forty times more Soviets than Americans died during the most ferocious and sustained campaign in military history. Let that sink in. Forty times more Soviets than Americans died during World War II. Almost all of European Russia was overrun, razed, and plundered. The entire Soviet infrastructure was destroyed, except the extraordinary wartime industrial complexes built to the east of the Volga and the Urals. Virtually every family lost a relative or close friend, many of them noncombatants. In short, WWII for European Russians was hell on earth.

Yet curiously, the U.S.S.R.'s victory in the Great Patriotic War—Russia's name for World War II—was the country's great defining moment under communism. The triumph over the Axis powers revalidated Stalin and 'the system' that had been so feared and discredited after the monstrous purges of the 1930s. The Soviets, for the first time, were united in a national purpose, and for a brief spell, up to Brezhnev, it looked as if the system would perpetuate itself.

As the decades passed and a younger generation grew up more interested in personal and economic freedoms, the flawed props underpinning the entire rotten Soviet state became increasingly evident. With the memory of the Great Patriotic War fading, a faltering economy, unattainable perks except for the opportunistic *nomenklatura*, the bloody and fruitless Afghan War, and finally closer access to the West, the Soviet state began its slow roll toward extinction.

SVETLANA

Svetlana is my sensibility barometer in Tver. During my summer studies in 1989, my primary instructor proved to be a fountain of practical knowledge about the U.S.S.R. She is a French professor and, in the Soviet era, could only dream of traveling to Paris and the Sorbonne for research. Ten years later, it was delightful to see Svetlana's animation when speaking of her three recent trips to Paris. She confesses, however, that life for her is much more complicated than before. She, in many ways, is experiencing the stressful life many professional women in the West live. Besides being a mother, she holds three jobs as professor, tutor, and researcher to supplement the $120 combined salary she and her husband, also a professor, draw from the University. She has taken up jogging to fight the stress.

Before the August 1998 ruble crisis, Svetlana had managed to build a comfortable lifestyle; at the time, the couple enjoyed a combined salary close to $1,000 a month. But her savings were hit hard in the devaluation, forcing her to postpone precious travel plans. One unanticipated positive result was that the expensive apartment she wanted to buy for her daughter suddenly became attainable. Originally priced at $12,000, the two-bedroom dwelling had been beyond Svetlana's means. When the real estate market in Tver collapsed after the 1998 devaluation, its price plummeted to $5,000. After learning that bank-supported home loans were pegged at about thirty-three percent annually, Svetlana turned to the so-called Barter Economy, which in her case meant the improvised and creative bartering of her services for a cash loan from friends. This bartering of services has been key in enabling the Russians to survive difficult times. She received the apartment money from friends and relatives and is now repaying them back $1,000 annually, as well as providing language lessons and research assistance to their children.

Svetlana, short and blond, was always an open-minded moderate concerning Russian life and politics. In 1989 she openly supported Gorbachev's reforms, voted for Yeltsin in 1992, and the liberal Yavlinsky in 1996. The following year, with Russia an economic mess and Tver rife with petty corruption, she probably would vote for the more conservative and stable Primakov, if he runs. She has no desire to vote the communists or any nationalists to power.

The NATO airstrikes against Yugoslavia in the spring and summer of 1999 really shook her. Like most Russians I talked to, Svetlana simply could not countenance NATO's violation of Yugoslavian territory, whatever the reason. It was the first time we had ever really disagreed on an issue. She is disappointed in the U.S. because she sees NATO as U.S.-led. She greatly dislikes Madeline Albright, who is regularly pilloried in the Russian press as a warmonger. I tried patiently to explain to her the U.S. view of why we and our European Allies simply could not tolerate such genocidal violence in Europe. We worried that the violence in Kosovo would spread throughout the Balkans. This point-of-view was difficult even for well-educated and open-minded Svetlana.[20]

Unlike the overwhelming majority of her age-group, Svetlana

is trying to adapt to the times. She works on an old 286 computer (introduced in the early 1980s) bought somehow for $500 several years ago. She covets access to the Internet but is not yet ready to pay the $50 to $60 required for a modem. She proudly showed me her computer-generated study plans that contrasted greatly with the mimeographed study sheets we worked off in 1989. In those days, a computer, let alone a photocopier, were absolutely unheard of in Kalinin. They were State-controlled items.

On Sundays during the summer, Svetlana travels out to her small *dacha* in an attempt to rest and see her family. Even then, she must take work with her. Her life has become so hectic that she cannot relax the entire weekend as she did in the old Soviet era. Still, she views those days as blessedly past.

Dachas play a very important role for the bulk of Russians who live in urban areas. The retreats, coupled with the barter economy, are an economic and social safety valve for the entire regime. When wondering how the Russians muddle through their food and grain shortages, remember the *dachas*. Most are small, unplumbed houses just outside the suburbs set in small forest communities alongside rivers and lakes. On weekends, families drive or take commuter trains out to these places to relax. On small, backyard plots they lovingly tend and harvest small crops of hardy produce ranging from cabbage, potatoes, radishes, cucumbers, beets, and other staples. Some, in improvised 'stills', produce *Samogon*, a high-octane spirit made out of anything distillable. Even in the darkest periods of the early 1990s, I was always amazed when visiting a home to be presented with trays full of summer produce. These garden supplements, often facilitated by barter and 'black untaxed labor', are among the key economic offsets that prop up the entire country and are a major reason why it is so difficult to accurately predict Russia's productivity, taxation, and employment. The *dachas* were important during last year's thirty percent drop-off in agricultural production and could become even more important this year (1999) considering the summer's drought and swarms of locusts.

Military

Beginning with my first visit in 1989, I have been treated repeatedly to a spectacle of a Soviet, then Russian, military in disarray. Despite the impressive, daily aerial flyby of the giant transport aircraft from Migelovo and the numerous officers seen in town, the closer one looked, the more one saw the tarnish. In 1989, I collected Russian military uniforms, trading away much of my own clothing to get difficult to obtain items. My New Balance running shoes netted me a full Spetsnaz (Soviet Special Forces) camouflage ensemble; my khakis and jeans brought me other neat stuff. This was a year or two before these uniforms started to be popular in the West.

One evening, I was taken by a friend to the decrepit Hotel Central, where he had befriended a Soviet Army Major who, quite furtively, wanted to sell me his entire uniform, along with various accouterments. Because I wouldn't pay with dollars, I gave him the Levi's I was wearing. (In the summer, I always wore a bathing suit underneath). I also promised to send him some medicine for his wife, which I did, but I don't know if he ever received it.

In November 1993, late one evening, I was hitchhiking back to my hotel and was picked up by a Russian Army jeep. In it was a young senior lieutenant on staff duty and his enlisted driver. Upon arrival at the hotel, he asked for two dollars, which I gave him—an action unimaginable today in our U.S. military culture.

Later, on a 1995 visit, I met a table-load of Russian officers from the Zhukov PVO (air defense) Academy who celebrated their graduation at the formerly strictly *apparatchik-mafia* Globus Restaurant. Sitting next to their raucous table, my friends and I decided to toast them. When the graduates learned I was a U.S. Army officer, they invited us to their table, and we were plied with food and excessive drink. After the usual comparisons of life and salaries, I had the most unusual conversation with a huge and absolutely intoxicated Air Force Lieutenant Colonel of

Armenian heritage who was piloting giant Antonov transports to Yerevan, Armenia's capital. In the spirit of camaraderie, he invited me along on one of his jaunts, which I politely told him I'd think about. I believe he was totally serious and his offer revealed yet another example of the ill-discipline and freelancing going on in the Russian military at the time.

As an epilogue to this story, I was later told by Tver locals about a terrible Air Force transport crash that occurred five years ago at Migelovo Airfield. The plane was rumored to be overloaded with Armenian passengers, foreign cars, furs, and generic contraband. This, of course, was during the height of the Nagorno-Karabakh crisis between Armenia and Azerbaijan and, if true, was yet another indicator of how deeply organized crime and corruption had permeated into many elements of the military.

One last observation about the Russian military. My Tver morning routine often begins with coffee and biscuits in a small cafe. In 1996, on two occasions, I saw Russian officers en route to the local Air Defense Academy publicly slamming back beers and a glass of vodka, respectively. This was at nine in the morning! All I know is that, despite our different military and societal differences, these types of behaviors do not indicate a healthy military culture when viewed as a whole do not indicate a healthy military culture.

Field Trips

WHILE STAYING IN KALININ/TVER THAT first summer of 1989, I met a group of historians who knew the ins and outs of Russian travel. From my good friend Ivan and his friends, we University students learned how to ride the superb Soviet mass transit system over hundreds of kilometers for mere pennies. Our basic rule in those days was that we would never overnight unofficially anywhere but Kalinin, in keeping with the spirit of our visa that limited us to the city. However, this caveat did not stop us from riding the rails from before dawn to beyond dusk within the robust commuter rail and river system that services a vast circle around Moscow.

For our first excursion, Ivan took me, along with my wonderful Tver roommate, Pennsylvania-born Brian Regli, on quite a naughty trip to the historic Napoleonic battlefield of Borodino, located one hundred twenty kilometers south of Moscow. Borodino was bloodily hallowed twice, in 1812 and again in 1941. To get there, we grabbed a filthy early *elektreechka* to Moscow, exited at the Leningrad station, zipped across Moscow on the best metro in the world to the Byelorussian railway station, hopped another *elektreechka* south to Mozhaysk, and piled into a desperately overcrowded country bus to Borodino (the *Vosmerka*—the #8). All this cost us less than a dollar. If we had traveled via Intourist, the trip would have been well over $100, even in 1989. Of course, all these switches took the better part of a day, but to travel without inordinate stress in Russia, one must be patient.

Standing amid the monuments and pillboxes of this blood-drenched battlefield, it was hard to imagine what business Napoleon's Grande Army had deep in Russia, more than a thousand miles northeast of Paris. Nonetheless, in one of the epic battles of the nineteenth century, Napoleon won a gruesome pyrrhic victory over his wily adversary Mikhail Kutuzov, losing a third of his Grande Army in the process. The rest of the story—the brief French occupation of Moscow and Napoleon's frozen retreat from Russia—is well-known history and memorialized by Tolstoy's *War and Peace* and Tchaikovsky's *1812 Overture*.[21]

The Soviet students, all steeped in Russian historiography, had a hidden motive for their visit. Standing next to the monument commemorating the valiant death of General Pyotr Bagration (who incidentally came from Georgian nobility), Ivan reached deep into his rucksack and pulled out the forbidden white, blue, and red flag of Imperial Russia, which only later, in 1991, was adopted by the new democratic republic. The students proudly, reverently, draped the flag over the monument, and we took pictures for them. It was a great moment.

We took another trip, this time trying out Central Russia's riverine transportation. We boarded a high-speed *Raket* river cruiser in Kalinin and, over several hours, zipped along the Volga and through canals and locks in a large man-made body of water known as the Moscow Sea. This extensive canal system was built in the 1930s by Soviet slave labor—tens of thousands of early political prisoners— during the first two Five Year Plans. Quite sophisticated for its time, the lock and river system linked Russia's inland waterways, allowing commerce to flow from Tver via Moscow all the way south to Astrakhan and the Caspian Sea—a distance of almost nine hundred miles.

Ivan also took me on the 'Gothic' tour of Tver and its environs. In 1996, we visited the Tver Institute of Medicine located, somewhat ironically, directly across Soviet Street from the Putevoy Palace—The Travel Palace. Formerly a Czarist-level school, it was converted in 1930 to an NKVD prison and became the key processing point for the thousands of unfortunate victims slated for liquidation during the Great Purge. After extracting false confessions for nebulous conspiracies against the State, often by torture, the victims were then loaded on trucks and transported to the rural village of Mednoye, about twenty-five kilometers north of Tver, where they were executed and buried.

We decided to visit Mednoye. By bus, we arrived in the village, and from the main highway, we followed on foot a dirt track that meandered several kilometers into a large birch forest. Along the way, we tore off and munched on chunks of black bread, my main Russian daytime staple, washing it down with distinctively salty Russian mineral water. In this quiet, idyllic setting, softened by the chirping of birds, we came upon the Mednoye killing field.

A simple monument stood over the large clearing inscribed "To the victims of the War and Repression."

Adjacent to this field was the site of an equally monstrous crime. In 1991, local Tver authorities finally admitted the existence of a large gravesite containing the bodies of more than 4,000 Polish officers rounded up after the German/Soviet invasion of Poland in 1939. This and another gravesite near Lake Ladoga, east of St. Petersburg, were directly linked to the Katyn Massacre, which occurred near Smolensk in 1940.

Mednoye is now a Polish national shrine and a commemorative plaque is affixed to the front façade of the Medical Institute in town, where many Poles were executed before burial in the forest. When we visited, the unmarked common graves were taped off, and Polish memorials—red and white flags and keepsakes—were spread among the trees which surrounded the remote location. Scattered about by visiting families were dozens of pictures of proud Polish officers resplendent in their distinctive uniforms. At the time those pictures were taken, none could have imagined the terrible fate that awaited them in this god-forsaken parcel of land in the heart of Mother Russia.

Adjacent to the combined gravesites is a large wooden house, built by the NKVD, practically on the bones of the thousands of deceased. Known today as the KGB Villa, it was used as a *dacha* for the NKVD and subsequently the KGB until 1991. It also, obviously, provided security for this gravesite, the existence of which was a Soviet state secret. (The Nazis discovered evidence of the Katyn massacre of Polish nationals during Barbarossa in 1941 and were promptly accused by the Soviets of killing the Poles. Revelations about Mednoye would have confirmed Nazi claims that the Soviets were the ones executing Polish officers. Of interest is the fact that in October 1941, the Germans were stopped by the Red Army at Mednoye as they pushed toward Moscow after capturing Kalinin and crossing the Volga. A huge propaganda victory would have been gained by the Germans if they had found additional mass Polish gravesites at Mednoye).[22]

While wandering around—we were the only visitors that day—we happened upon a very old Russian woman from Kazakhstan who now lived in the KGB Villa. She had been given the villa to tend in 1993. The woman broke into tears when we asked her about the grim events that occurred there from 1936-

1941. She had lost her own grandfather during that horrible period. Short of the self-consuming purges that wracked the NKVD (revolutions and purges invariably eat their own), there was never any real effort to bring the perpetrators of The Great Purge to justice. In Tver Oblast alone, there must have been dozens of residents who were directly involved in the murders— and many more who knew of them. Some probably still lived nearby.

I harp on this period because I believe that even today, the ghastly events that happened 60 years ago are still etched in the Russian mind and are reflected in their voting behavior. As one old-timer related to me his reason for voting for Yeltsin over Zyuganov: "People don't like the Mafia but dislike the NKVD even more!"

Timur and Darya

THE SOMBERNESS OF VISITING MEDNOYE was, fortunately, more than balanced by the rural pleasure I've enjoyed for ten years during delightful visits with a family who lives in a regional sovkhoz, a collective farm. I first met Timur and his wife Darya on a 1989 'folk night' arranged for our University group. They had recently settled there from Baku, capital of the Azerbaijani Republic, which had become unstable and dangerous. Timur looked anything but ethnically Azerbaijani. He was tall, blond, blue-eyed, and possessed a powerful body that looked sculpted right out of a Grecian martial statue. Darya, in contrast, was classic Azerbaijani: tall, dark, and fiery. Both were teachers. Timur was the sovkhoz school's physical education teacher, and Darya had taught herself enough English to become an English teacher.

I visited them several times in 1989, twice for tennis duels with Timur on an ersatz tennis court painted on the parking lot in front of the collective farm's schoolhouse. It is hard to imagine Timur before his marriage and quiet life near Tver. From 1983 to 1985, he was an elite Soviet Airborne Sergeant in a special operations unit (Spetsnaz) who admitted 'bagging' a number of Afghan mujahideen during the difficult fighting. He himself was shot through the leg in 1985 during a well-laid Afghan ambush near Herat, in which several of his friends were killed. He only talks about Afghanistan when I ask him questions. In a later meeting, he gave me his uniform and airborne beret, which I know were very personal to him.

Darya and Timur have raised a lovely family. Their two beautiful daughters, Masha and Irina, greet me as DaDa Pyotr (Uncle Peter) and love to try out their schoolgirl English on me. Masha enjoys video movies; in fact, at the precocious age of ten, her favorite two films are *Dirty Dancing* and *Titanic*, both in English. Who says U.S. culture hasn't penetrated deep into Russia?

I always bring a gift. This year it was two Barbie-type dolls, which were a big hit with the girls. Toys in Russia ten years ago were so simple. So much has changed in Russia since 1989. Notably, almost every single school teaches some English, which in half a generation and ten more years of Internet connections will become the second language of Russia.

The emergency ruble devaluation in 1998 also hit the sovkhoz hard. Timur had supplemented his $150 a month income with several other enterprises, including a weekly drive to Smolensk with a truckload of imported goods routed via Tver. Darya also made about $150 a month, so last summer, before the devaluation, they together earned close to $1,000 a month—not bad at all considering that their rent and electric bill was fifty rubles ($2) and sixty rubles ($2.50) respectively.

Low rents are typical in Russia. People would simply not be able to afford higher. Other costs, however, have gone up. For instance, regular gasoline costs about forty percent more now—up to 4.5 to five rubles a liter, equating to about eighty cents a gallon. Typical bread went up to three rubles (fifteen cents) from two (ten cents), and a pack of Timur's preferred Soyuz-Apollo cigarettes doubled. All these prices seem absurdly cheap until one steps back and realizes that the typical pensioner is given only $60 monthly.

The greatest setback for the family was that they had to shelve their plans to visit the French Disney World this year. Their cost would have been $350 apiece (x4) to take a long two-day bus ride to Paris and spend five days on-site. That they could even consider the trip was amazing; it would have been inconceivable just two years ago. I didn't have the heart to tell them that my own family had sailed on the *Disney Magic* just a month before.

Over a delicious lamb pilaf laced with apricots, the three of us discussed the state of Russia and the world. Darya admitted that their family felt mild ostracism in their collective for being Azerbaijani. Even so, it did not hold them back, because Timur is now under consideration to be the school principal. More hardline than her husband, Darya was very uncomfortable with NATO's bombing of Yugoslavia, a recurring theme I heard everywhere I went, even among the calmest and sober Russians.

Timur and Darya, along with my teacher Svetlana, always give me perspective and balance when I visit Tver. They are the stable baseline from which I peer through my personal window into provincial Russia's heart, soul and psyche.

IVAN

I MET IVAN IN 1989, during my first stay in Tver, and our mutual love of history has kept us in close contact during subsequent visits. Blond, blue-eyed, intense and slight of stature, Ivan is evolving into one of Russia's leading historians and heraldic experts. Poorly paid as a professor (about $100 per month), he is able to supplement his salary through his burgeoning heraldic research, which includes finding the long-lost and forgotten medieval coats-of-arms for cities willing to pay for his skills. Ivan is a proud Russian nationalist who was an absolute Monarchist in 1989 and believed Russia needed to return to its Orthodox roots and a Czar. Since then, his views have mellowed somewhat to a more benign nationalism—not the ignorant Zhirinovsky type, which he views as a clown—but he believes ardently that the Ukraine and Byelorussia should be again part of 'Imperial' Russia. He shares the pathological fear many Russians have of China. While discussing my 1997 trip to the Russian Far East he commented: "The nine million white Russians who live between Irkutsk and Vladivostok are not captives, but they live like *Dekabristi* (Czarist nineteenth-century exiles to Siberia) because they live next to a billion Chinese!"[23]

Ivan has a visceral distrust of NATO and is unsure about the U.S.-Russian partnership—views which always made for spicy conversations and repartees between us. Our political and strategic discussions would usually end in stalemate, and then we would switch gears and talk about what we enjoyed most: history.

Ivan managed to travel to Milan (Italy) and Switzerland and was absolutely amazed by Swiss cleanliness. His charming wife Natasha is a research assistant who earns about half of Ivan's pay. His marvelously wise and clear-headed eighty-six-year-old grandmother perfectly epitomizes the Soviet/Russian experience. Her vision was refreshing when contrasted with the standard Western stereotype of old pro-Communist Russian pensioners. She was a construction engineer in the prewar U.S.S.R. and lost her husband early in the war. In fact, both Ivan's and Natasha's grandfathers died in WWII. Sadly, such losses became the norm rather than the exception in the war-torn U.S.S.R. She admitted that life was easier and less complicated under Communism; however, she is happy they are gone and voted for the reformer Yavlinsky in the 1996 election.[24] At the time I'm writing this, she is undecided for 2000.

I asked her why she voted for the liberals. She looked at me with clear, calm eyes that almost twinkled and simply said, "za budushchee" ("For the future.") I ran into this phenomenon time and again during my travels in Russia. The older pensioners are not a monolithic bloc, although the seventy-five percent ruble devaluation of August 17, 1998, hurt them profoundly.

Let me share with you what my friend Larissa told me about that horrible August day.

Larisa woke up to find long lines queued up to the bank near her home. She called a friend who saw the same thing in her neighborhood. She came out in the street with no clue of what to do. Many middle-aged and elderly residents were already in long lines in front of commodity stores, buying up everything they could. Larissa and many of her younger friends were in a panic. It seemed Tver was unraveling in front of their eyes.

What happened in Tver was indicative of the angst that pervaded Russia that day. When the devaluation was announced, there was a run on banks, most of which closed their doors. Many stores and kiosks remained shut for several days as the ruble gyrated wildly between twenty-five and forty percent of its former value. Those stores that remained open had only a few staples—repetitive rows of jarred cabbage and older produce. Larissa could not even find a tube of toothpaste. The paradox here was that the older people immediately went back to their old Soviet ways: they got in line and bought and hoarded all the commodities they could afford.

The younger adults, those under thirty-five years old really, were genuinely scared. They had never experienced such a scenario before. Luckily, Larisa and her young friends all had a good proportion of their savings in dollars and rode out the financial crisis. Others were not so lucky. Small businesses with savings in rubles were shattered. The worst hit, as always, were the pensioners and workers, many of whom were already not being paid on time and now faced additional financial stress.[25]

Amazingly, the Russians once again somehow adjusted to this crisis and aftermath without taking to the streets. If one visited Tver today, one year later, you would never know how close to economic and financial meltdown Russia was last year. The streets are bustling, more stores and restaurants continue to open, and higher quality goods, both foreign and Russian, fill the stores. Yet everyone is a little bit poorer, save for the crooks, businessmen, and companies that work in dollars. Up until August 1998, a solid majority of Russians would have said, if asked, that life was getting slowly better. Fewer would say that today and many covet the apparent wealth and power of Mayor Igor Luzhkov's Moscow, which is said to generate or attract up to sixty percent of Russia's entire Gross National Product.

Other, more enlightened people say that the collapse was the shock therapy that Russia needed and never undertook voluntarily, unlike neighboring Poland, whose economy continues to briskly grow after bottoming out in the early 1990s.

One thing is certain: Dissecting and explaining this crisis and related economic activities will be the central event affecting Russian voting behavior in 2000.

IGOR

IGOR LAY IN A SINGLE hospital bed with a blood drip attached and a used bedpan sitting on a chair next to him. Around him, jammed into the small room, were eight other patients, some with bloody bandages wrapped around their torsos, lying mostly on top of their beds in the summer heat. The smell of sweat and lye permeated the room. Hospital #7 clearly worked hard to be clean but had little of the technology and sanitation we are accustomed to in our own country. I wondered how the patients survived at night in the heat with the screen-less windows open. They appeared to be ripe meat for Tver's voracious mosquitoes.

Looking wan, Igor was surprised, happy, and seemingly embarrassed to see me. He was missing a tooth since I last saw him. We talked for a few minutes about old times, and then he asked that I leave. He did not want me to see him in this condition, in these circumstances. I gave him a hug and some photos I had taken of us together and left.

Igor had a bleeding ulcer and had been admitted to the hospital for the second time in six months. Told to stop drinking vodka, he didn't listen and had fallen unconscious in the nightclub where he worked. He was hauled off by ambulance just a day before I was to meet him. I literally learned Igor's sorry story from the club's door-woman after arriving in Tver the night after the episode.

The club itself has an interesting story. It was converted from the former Kalinin Soviet Officer's Club, a revealing sign of how far the stature of the military has fallen. In 1996 it was even used for a 'congress' of Chechen deputies as well as being a nightclub.

Igor is my closest friend in Tver. Considered a ne'er-do-well by many, he nonetheless provided me an absolutely unique, fascinating, and at times downright hilarious view of Tver and Russian life. In spite of being very well-educated, Igor drifted from job to job, mostly linked to the entertainment business. In the ten years I've known him, he has worked as a DJ, a T-shirt silk-screen printer, a manager for his friend who ran ice cream kiosks and commodities, gym manager for the Proletarka martial arts center, a DJ again and finally, an assistant manager at the Officer's Nightclub. He knew everybody and everything in Tver and took me all over the place.

We met through the University in 1989 when my group was invited to see the Kalinin branch of the Central Army Hockey team. He was the team's marketer and befriended several of us, students, soon arranging for riotous inebriated midnight hockey games without skates on Tver center ice. After careening around the ice, we (about six of us students, some hockey players, and Igor) would then pile into the large sauna, baths, and cooling tubs, which made up the team's clubhouse. We would stay there almost all night, walking out into Kalinin's permanent early morning summer twilight, and would struggle through our morning Russian language classes.

Most memorably, Igor showed me Kalinin's/Tver's 'dirty petticoats'. Igor was charismatic and a ladies' man. Tall, lanky, he sported a long ponytail until 1997. If he had had a long beard, he would have looked a bit like Rasputin. His absolutely charming and gorgeous Kalinin girlfriend later became a prostitute in Moscow before returning to Tver to marry a local boy to raise a family (Much as Marina was seduced by Chechen money, this was not unfamiliar and unacceptable activity). Igor then married a Ukrainian woman from Tarnopol twenty years younger who drank almost as much as he did. Their relationship was stormy and brief. Both ladies still have affection for Igor as a friend because, despite his many glaring foibles, he is a fundamentally decent and gentle guy.

I also met Igor's friend Rudik. He deserves a short story by himself. Rudik is a portly, middle-aged Armenian who settled in Tver with his large family in a worker's district near Proletarka. He made his living by trading in trousers that he pulled in from all over the former Soviet Union. One dark evening in the winter of 1991, Igor, Rudik, and I were sitting in the sports club's baths, drinking vodka with several hockey players and some of their young sports groupies. Rudik in the buff displayed a shocking scar, almost a cavity, in his very hairy midriff. He had been shot during the Armenian-Azerbaijani bloodletting in Nagorno-Karabakh that began in 1988.[26] As the evening wore on, he became obnoxious in an affable kind of way until he, being the Caucasus chauvinist he was, started trying to grope the poor young ladies in the massive hot tub we were in. We dragged him out of the tub before the hockey players killed him, and I took him out into the street to find him a car home. Because I had taken a personal interest in his welfare, he then insisted on escorting ME instead for MY safety to the Motel Tver, the overpriced Intourist establishment on the edge of town. (Once a friend of Rudik, you are a friend for life.)

When we got there, Rudik insisted on another drink, and then another in the all-night bar. While I was trying to urge him out of the Motel lobby, he sat down like a Buddha and started to sing the most plaintive songs I have ever heard—songs from deep in his native Armenian mountains. I apologized for him to the night clerk, the security people and Alex's kiosk salesperson (I had a good rapport with them) and asked them to be patient with him as he was not harming anyone. Finally, at dawn, I bade Rudik good night. I was exhausted and exasperated by his antics. He apparently stayed put, entertaining the staff until nine that morning, before staggering home. I ran into Rudik the following summer. He was shy and circumspect. We never mentioned the incident.

I stayed at the suburban Motel Tver every visit until 1993 when I switched to the Hotel Volga. The Motel had an interesting clientele because it catered to Russian traffic, especially Finnish truckers and tour buses, traveling on the main highway between Moscow and St. Petersburg. It was at the Motel Tver in 1990 that I screwed up my courage, hired a local car for fifteen dollars, and drove one hundred eighty kilometers through the U.S.S.R. to Moscow. This was back when road traffic was still somewhat regulated.

In true adventure mode and with some Soviet driving experience under my belt, the following summer with my good friend Ralph Peters, author and fellow Foreign Area Officer, I somehow rented a sturdy Lada in Moscow. We proceeded to drive more than three thousand, one hundred miles over erratic roads from Moscow via Tula, Kursk, Kharkov, Eastern Ukraine, Rostov, and over the Georgian Military Highway to Tbilisi, and finally to the Sochi seaside. That was during the waning months of the Soviet Union, the summer of 1991. It was a memorable trip. In the Caucasus mountains, we crossed over some roads that were still closed since the bloody civil fighting in South

Ossetia the previous winter. The highlight of our trek was a drive, cable car, and hike to the summit of Mount Elbrus, the tallest mountain in Europe.

One of the few times I ever felt under observation was at the Motel Tver. My first summer back in Tver—1990—a college friend of mine named Yevgeni was working in an adjacent trailer park. I used to come over to talk to him on my way in and out of town. One day he told me that the local security guy at the Motel had pulled him aside, asking if he knew I was a U.S. Army officer. It was no secret, so he told the security hack yes and was never bothered about it again. The following year my Russian visa photo was disconnected from the visa form, which caused me grief and a twenty-dollar 'fine' levied by a young, green-tabbed Soviet KGB guard—the Soviet 'elite'—at passport control did not give me a receipt for the paid fine.

As recently as this past summer, the Russian authorities, citing safety, tried to book me from Washington, D.C. into the Motel Tver for seventy-eight dollars a night. Tourists must still pre-buy hotel rooms before receiving a visa unless they're lucky enough to have an 'invitation.' This was ridiculous and indicative that some of the old ways still live on. I changed the reservation upon reaching Moscow and moved to the roughly equivalent Hotel Volga for eight dollars a night. Enough said

FRIENDS

OTHER RUSSIAN FRIENDS NOT PROFILED separately in this story peeled off into all sorts of work and experiences. One of the nicest, Marina, was a tall, young University of Kalinin escort who became one of our closest friends. In 1991 she moved to Moscow. Ralph and I found her the following year at the notoriously tacky Arlekino discotheque, sitting with several Chechen mobsters.[27] I went up to kiss her hello and was met with a scared look from her and a cold-blooded, menacing stare from the Chechens. I backed off. She apparently had been enticed by easy money and the prospect of a swank lifestyle outside of Tver and had become a 'kept woman' with the Chechensi (slang for Chechens) for about two years before breaking free, marrying a Mercedes-driving financial broker and building a family.

Marina's best friend in 1989 was a gorgeous extrovert who we named 'Olga from the Volga.' Olga spoke perfect English, was brilliant, and captivated every foreign male within eye-shot. She wasted no time getting out of the U.S.S.R. When I returned to Tver the following summer, she had already been snapped up by a Belgian and whisked away to a new home near Antwerp.

I also was introduced at a picnic at a local lake to a tight trio of friends, Raisa, Larisa, and Anna. The meeting was made especially memorable by an encounter I had with a drunk, obnoxious, nationalist Russian, who insisted on challenging me, an American, to a swimming race. I swam while he flailed across the lake, almost drowning in the process.

The three young ladies were all philology students in 1989, studying mostly English and some German. Raisa married an artist, Yuri, from Moscow, who paints those wonderful black lacquer boxes, the best being known as *Palekh*. One evening at Yuri's studio, he showed me the painstaking labor that goes into painting a Russian fairy tale on each box. It was fascinating to see him with the tiniest of brushes paint the boxes with brilliant colors, highlight each with gilt, and finish with a patina of clear lacquer.[28] They were able to move to Amsterdam in 1997—another Tverite family flown the coop.

By 1999, the trio had gone different ways. The last time I saw the trio together was when we met the drunken Soviet graduating officers at the Mafiosi restaurant Globus in 1995.

Larissa remained in Tver and is now a very strict English teacher at the University. Precise and well-organized, she is the model of efficiency and manages her teaching while raising a pretty little daughter. Her teaching salary approaches about eighty dollars, thanks to having a little tenure in the University. Her husband, a lawyer for the nearly bankrupt Tver Universal Bank, provides her a decent living, though she is troubled by side businesses he does not want to tell her about.

Anna, the youngest of the group, has blossomed into an interesting woman in her own right. For the last three years, she has been working as an escort in a dating/marriage service set up by a firm in California. Tver apparently is a popular way-station for Russian women desperate to find a U.S. husband and leave Russia and has also been discovered by U.S. men who for whatever reason can't find the women they want in the U.S. Three competing dating agencies have set up in Tver.

While eating dinner with my philosopher friend Vadim in the new Hotel Osnabruck (Osnabruck being Tver's sister city), I noticed a rather awkward foreigner sitting with two Russian women. It became clear that he was an American because they helped him count out his money and change. He had just given his Russian date flowers, and as they passed the table where we were eating, I caught the clenched, set look on the potential bride's face as meaning "I will somehow endure this."

Anna's job as an escort is to be the linguistic go-between for the American man and Russian woman, both of whom rarely speak each other's language. This was an important job because the typical client paid anywhere between $3,000 and $5,000 to travel to Russia and be set up for up to two weeks in a Tver apartment in order to review files and go out on a series of dates. The results were tragi-comedy. First, as an escort, Anna had to interject herself into every conversation from the most mundane to the most intimate, short of a direct sexual proposition.

She would even walk them up together to an apartment for a connubial evening.

Most of the U.S. clients were decent and well-behaved while in Russia. However, some became chauvinistic monsters when they returned to the States with the captive bride in hand. Other brides discarded their men after a brief hiatus in the U.S. Still, other suitors, tired or frustrated with the hunt, asked Anna if she could arrange prostitutes for them, which her company did as a courtesy. The cost in Tver averaged about fifty dollars, which was a bargain when compared to Moscow's two hundred dollar standard. In contrast, street prostitutes in Tver, a city with the fourth highest AIDS rate in Russia, score two dollars for oral sex and about five dollars for an hour of sex.

Because Anna is rather fetching herself and speaks excellent English, more than a few of the clients tried to propose to her instead. One man of Portuguese descent broke into tears upon Anna's gentle rejection and disappeared for several days, which absolutely unhinged the agency, fearful that he had taken his life out of despair. Later he called from the States to say he was OK and asked to have his bags forwarded.

For her work Anna receives five dollars a day from her agency; what she relies on are often considerable tips from satisfied clients. This business for U.S. men is the rage in Russia right now. One can now also see sizable numbers of Russian prostitutes in every major city in the liberal world today.

Through Anna, I learned that the swank (for Tver) Oasis Club, clearly a Mafia establishment, was off-limits to Americans during NATO's bombing campaign against Yugoslavia. She also said that she was occasionally contacted by the FSB, today's KGB, about her clients. She bet me that she would get a call about me. I accepted the bet and said, if they do call, to please tell them everything we talked about. Hopefully, our conversation would spice up their dreary routine.

FUTURE

THE POLITICAL PROGNOSIS FOR THE 2000 presidential elections is very hazy when viewed from Tver. While the democratic process remains important for the majority of Tverites, most have essentially tuned out the day-to-day histrionics and capricious governmental shuffles in Moscow. Virtually all believe that Boris Yeltsin must go. They are looking for a man to bring order, reduce corruption and encourage economic stability to the troubled land. The bottom line fact is that living conditions—although cosmetically better—still are at subsistence level or worse for most Russians. Their ruble is broken, and the country is at war on its periphery.

Risking both boredom and boordom, I asked everyone I met in Tver on this trip about their perspective on the upcoming

2000 political election. Most are numb after six successive Prime Ministers and four full changes of government within eighteen months. The following is an amalgam of their views:

The usual field of candidates is changing because Yeltsin is not permitted to run for a third presidential term. Yevgeny Primakov is picking up support in Tver as a no-nonsense, tough, and experienced politician with an honest reputation.[29] His seven-month tenure as Prime Minister after the chaotic ruble devaluation in 1998 was seen as calming by most Russians. Little does it matter to most that he was a dedicated Soviet Cold War era diplomat and spymaster with good, anti-U.S. links to some rogue states in the Middle East.

Another man to watch is Igor Luzhkov, Big Boss and mayor of Moscow in the best spirit of former Mayor Daley of Chicago. Luzhkov, a dynamo, has put Moscow back on the face of the cosmopolitan world with an extraordinary construction and growth spurt. At the same time, he is purported to be the supra-organized crime *capo* of the city, reigning over it like a feudal lord. He can get away with this since he sports about an eighty-five percent approval rating, thanks to cleaning up most of the petty crime in the Moscow area. He will be one to watch for 2000, especially in coalition with some of the former aggrieved Prime Ministers.[30]

There also is talk of Yeltsin unwisely abolishing the Communist Party. Its leader, Gennady Zyuganov, was a potent challenger to Yeltsin in 1996, winning Tver by three percent. The centrist communist will run again, although it appears that his appeal is fading, as his increasingly elderly constituency also fades away. Also, a Primakov candidacy could draw supporters from Zsuganov's ranks.

The ultra-nationalist Vladimir Zhirinovsky will pick up his few percent of the votes but is not taken seriously by most Russians. Tverites still remember his outrageous visit in 1996 that culminated in a sour exchange in a local news interview and a resultant water fight.

General Lebed, Governor of Krasnoyarsk District in Siberia, has marginalized himself somewhat by not building up an auspicious legislative or performance record in the hinterland. He is a nationalist 'law and order' wild-card, however, and could be someone to be reckoned with if Russians become disenchanted by the way things are going in the Balkans or in Russia's Muslim province of Dagestan.

There are even more candidates to consider: the stolid Viktor Chernomyrdin, Mr. GAZPROM (Russian Oil Ministry), who is allegedly the richest man in Russia and twice Prime Minister within the last eighteen months,[31] or, a combination of Sergei Kirilenko[32] or Sergei Stepashin,[33] two other Prime Ministers since March 23, 1998.

There is also the longtime reformer, Gregor Yavlinsky, who is seen by many Russians as influential and important—but ultimately a wasted vote in this important election. One well-educated acquaintance said of the largely incorruptible Yavlinsky, "I don't trust him; he's Jewish."

The 2000 election will be decisive for Russia and the direction it navigates in the first decade of the next millennium. The country stands at a crossroads, much as Weimar Germany did in the 1920s. It can move forward in its reforms and build on its still fledgling eight-year-old democratic system, or it can take the easier route and revert to a more authoritarian system. The run-up to the election will be a pivotal year in which much more can go wrong than go right. Voting to retain a fully democratic system that one day will be accountable to the Russian citizens will be a great challenge of almost superhuman patience for the exhausted, apathetic, and financially broken mainstream population. Hearteningly, even now, many recognize there is no alternative but to continue to press ahead.

Goodbye Tver

On my last day in Tver in the summer of 1999, I tried to visit stricken Igor again to give him some extra cash and to say goodbye. To my consternation, I learned that an ambulance moved him that week to a hospital outside of Tver for further treatment, which meant that his condition had worsened. Recovery can take a long time in the creaky Russian medical system.

Late that final afternoon, I went back to the little parcel of land that I call a beach on the Volga's south shore to write notes and to take a last swim in the slow-flowing river. As always, the water was opaque but invigorating. Upon hauling myself out of the river, I stood up to my hips in the shallows, squeezing the muddy, pumice-like silt between my toes. To the left and right, children were squealing their delight as they charged into the sluggish water while others floated about on rubber rafts. Their parents, a few dressed like Amagansett yuppies, shouted their encouragement and caution from the embankment where I used to play chess ten years before. A militiaman, dressed in his gray uniform and forage cap strode by and sat down in the shade. He ignored the several adults approaching from the opposite bank. Obviously, he was in no mood to enforce the Volga no-crossing rule.

I must have stood there for over an hour, enjoying the balmy late afternoon sun while reflecting on my trips to Tver and the future of Russia. At last, I gathered up my notes from the beach and headed slowly toward the Hotel Volga. As I walked, I realized something was missing. In 1989, the noise of the nearby airbase had been relentless—a constant reminder of Russia's longstanding military mindset.

Now I scanned the unusually quiet sky.

Not an airplane in sight.

Fin

Afterword

THIRTEEN YEARS AFTER WHAT I thought was my final visit to
Kalinin-Tver, I serendipitously returned to the small city in 2012
to attend a one-week U.S. Embassy program on Russian language
and culture. Some, though fewer and fewer, U.S.-Russian cultural
exchanges like this occurred until relations collapsed in 2014. By
then, I had been promoted to the rank of Brigadier General—
something I never imagined—and held the post of the Senior
U.S. Defense Official and Attaché to the Russian Federation —
an assignment I never dreamed of as a young military officer,
certainly not during my initial visits to Kalinin-Tver[34] more than
two decades earlier.

For me, the 2012 visit was a bit of a homecoming. I was able
to work in several little reunions with some of my old Kalinin

friends. Given my rank and position at the time, reconnecting with my old friends might have been awkward. But I had never made a secret of my military career and had also dropped in occasionally for visits through the years. Because we never delved into details of my career or sensitive Russian topics, our friendships were open, easygoing, and based on fond memories of local excursions and many late-night conversations over assorted "*zakuski*" lubricated by vodka shots.

On my 2012 visit, I was—as always—struck by how much Tver had changed during my absences. Tver and other small cities outside of the sprawling Moscow metropolitan area were slowing modernizing. (The more rural settlements and regions have not kept pace, however.) Old cash registers and even some abacus prevalent during my first visits to the city had been replaced by cash ATMs and credit cards. The Internet was everywhere and, in spite of growing governmental controls, the city's youth could link easily to the outside world. A few of my Tver pals are even Facebook friends with me—an amazing development.

More changes were visible in visits after 2012 too. (My last one took place in 2019.) The renovation of old Russian Orthodox churches continues apace, and new churches are being built. Catherine the Great's "Travel Palace" (mentioned in my diary) has been beautifully restored. The Old Soviet trolleys and *elektreechka* commuter trains have been modernized with new German-Russian "*Lastochka*" (Swallow) trains and the ticket system has been digitized. Mostly privately-owned vehicles of both Russian and foreign makes cruise the streets.

The passage of the years had brought changes to my friends too. Students I had met when they were in their twenties were now seasoned adults in their forties and fifties. Alex and Sasha had financially benefited from seizing opportunities in the wide-open 1990s. Artur had moved to Seattle and became a successful American businessman. Ivan became the top heraldry expert in the region. Timur and Darya, now with fully grown daughters, continue to teach from their collective farm. Larissa became a serious language professor at the University. Sadly, my Tver running-buddy Igor died an alcoholic, way too young, in his early fifties.

Kseniya, who saw me swept downriver in the swollen Volga during one of my swims, currently lives comfortably with family in Moscow. The fresh-faced, innocent Marina from Kalinin State University, who I last saw in the company of the Chechen Mafia in 1993, simply disappeared. Russia's changeover from a landline telephone system to cellular made it impossible to trace some people, including Anna and Svetlana, my original and very wise teacher in 1989. Several other teachers from my first summer in Kalinin have passed on.

In 2013, I had the joy of bringing my family to Tver by train on the same route that brought me to Kalinin 24 years earlier. Friends met us at the rail station and escorted us through the forest to their home. A recent foot operation required me to do the walk—slowly—with a crutch. When we arrived at the house, the grizzled grandfather (*dedushka*) spied my bandaged foot and gave me his version of physical therapy: a rough, countryside foot massage that had me wincing. With a crooked grin he asked me "am you crying yet?" but actually made my foot feel noticeably better for several weeks. In a surreal "*déjà vu*" we stayed in the renovated Hotel Volga, where I had summered with my American classmates almost a quarter of a century earlier. In a particularly lovely moment, I took my family to my favorite stretch of the

Volga, the riverbank, where we spent so much time in the summer of 1989. This time I swam in the river wearing an American USO hat, thoroughly enjoying the memories.

The 2013 trip was especially meaningful because it brought me closure and full circle. And just in time, too. When Russia invaded Ukraine and backed Syria's strongman Bashar al-Assad the following year, most travel and exchanges came to a halt. Relations between Russia and the West have remained frosty ever since.

The deterioration of relations, while always edgy, has been hard to watch. When the U.S.S.R. formally broke apart in 1991, anything seemed possible. U.S. popularity in post-Soviet Russia soared to unforeseen heights. The average Russians I met were open to exploring capitalism and modernization. But the world—and Moscow too—somehow fumbled a golden opportunity to welcome a traumatized but curious Russia into the mainstream family of cooperating nations. Instead, always proud Russia soon turned inward and nursed assorted grievances, real and imagined, against the West—a global failure of the first order. Resentment, suspicion, and distrust once again appear to guide Russia's foreign policy.

The country's internal challenges have only added to the problems. The economic sanctions imposed by the West after the Ukraine invasion in 2014 contributed to an inflation crisis and curtailed the availability of many products. Although the inflation problem has calmed down, the buying power and value of the ruble to the dollar is still about half of what it was when I served in Moscow from 2012 to 2014. Even so, for typical Russian citizens, quality of life is still better and more stable than it was during the chaos of the 1990s. Creative workarounds have developed in every sector, from banking to food. A proliferation of homemade vegetable-and-fruit producing greenhouses softens the impact on the population somewhat. Despite recent increases, low oil prices persist, slowing development and modernization. There is less of everything, especially quality foodstuffs, but enough to go around.

For the moment, Russia appears to be muddling through; even so, the so-called 'social contract' between the regime in Moscow and the Russian people seems to be fraying. The mainstream population mostly tolerates the easily-observed corruption within the regime, as long as there is a perception in the hinterland that the quality of life will still slowly improve. But signs of restlessness and dissatisfaction can be seen. The ongoing anti-corruption demonstrations orchestrated by dissidents such as the imprisoned Alexei Navalny, plus the shock of mandated later retirement ages for millions of pensioners, hint that the people are growing impatient with the status quo.

My primary concern is Russia's longstanding defensive attitude toward its neighbors. During more than three decades of studying Russia's history and visiting the country, I believe that Russia lives in a self-imposed world of existential threats, real, perceived—and also, very importantly—contrived, in a way that is difficult for those of us in the U.S. and West to fully understand. A vivid example is Russia's visceral negative perception of NATO's enlargement to the east in recent years. I have tried repeatedly in conversations with Russians to explain how critical it was to pull an anxious and distressed Eastern Europe together into a mutually beneficial security structure after the Cold War—and as such is no threat to Russia—but my explanation is usually met with skepticism and suspicion.

After my most recent trips to Russia and Tver between 2016

and 2019, I've become quite concerned by the even greater and more dangerous trust deficit between Russia and the U.S.—the two most lethally equipped nuclear powers in the world. The lack of trust between the two countries has not eased one iota since the dramatic events of 2014 when Russia's invasion of the Ukraine and actions in Syria provoked a global outcry and international sanctions. In fact, the relationship continued to deteriorate after the discovery that Russia repeatedly interfered with the U.S. electoral process in 2016 and that the Colonial Pipeline ransomware attack in May 2021 originated on Russian soil. Diplomacy between NATO and Russia is at a chilly standstill. Our militaries constantly brush up against one another in Eastern Europe and elsewhere on the globe, keeping tensions high.

The greatest danger from my perspective is the possibility of a blindingly quick accident or incident that rapidly escalates into a military confrontation that no one wants. It's not as far-fetched as you might think. The window for making heat-of-the-moment decisions has decreased dramatically. Our hard-won Cold War era arms treaties fell away one by one in recent years, endangering a carefully crafted system of communications and mutual checks designed to reduce the possibility of misunderstandings. In 2019, for example, we lost the 1987 Intermediate Nuclear Forces (INF) Treaty. Other treaties lapsed even earlier. One bright spot is the recent five-year extension of the strategic nuclear New START Treaty—a development that could help to slow any renewed nuclear arms race and address dangerous new technologies such as artificial intelligence and a dangerous new generation of weapons led by hypersonic missiles.

Perhaps the greatest source of future problems for Russia will, in fact, turn out to be a very old problem: geography. Unless you take the time to look carefully at a globe or map, it's easy to miss the key fact that Russia spills across eleven time zones—almost halfway around the world. Yet it has only 40 percent the population of the U.S., one-third of the European Union's and a mere one-ninth of neighboring behemoth China. (China shares a border with Russia on par with our U.S. border with Canada.) The magnitude of Russia's geographic sprawl, lightly guarded borders and relatively small population, has long fueled a level of paranoia and defensiveness that few other nations can grasp. During a memorable visit to Russia's Far Eastern region in 2000,

I stood on the country's border and peered across the Tumen River south of Vladivostok into North Korea—an experience that underscored to me the importance of viewing the vastness of Eurasian Russia from a Globalist's perspective.

Although Russia has reveled in the U.S. and coalition defeat in Afghanistan during August 2021, their diplomatic behavior since the withdrawal reveals that the country recognizes that its vast southern flank is now more vulnerable without the physical presence of the U.S. and allies in the region. The Central Asia region as a whole is threatened by the prospect of a volatile and unstable Afghanistan in the hands of the Taliban, a situation that could easily spark another Civil War. The furies of jihadism, drugs, crime and unfettered migration might well spill through the region into southern Russia and the Caucasus, a shared concern that might shift U.S.-Russian relations. The Soviet's own decade-long (1989-1999) failure to subdue Afghanistan is still recent enough to inspire caution and negative reactions from embittered Russian soldiers in that expensive and exhausting campaign. I got an earful from disillusioned veterans in 1989 when I studied in Tver, also site of a major military airbase. More than twenty years later, after my own military service in Afghanistan (2008-2009), I often spoke with my Russian counterparts about their experiences and more than once attended solemn events commemorating their sacrifices.

What particularly concerns me now, in 2021, is the lack of direct communication between Russia's leaders and ours. Few senior leaders of either country—including military leaders—are routinely talking to each other right now. The U.S. Chairman of the Joint Chiefs and the Russian Chief of the General Staff occasionally meet, but subordinate commanders and staffs worldwide do not. It would be difficult to de-escalate a dangerous situation when the world's two biggest nuclear powers are barely in contact. You certainly don't want opposing senior regional military leaders and their staffs trying to get to know each other during a cyber-fast breaking crisis far from Moscow, Washington, D.C. or Brussels. That kind of critical groundwork needs to happen well ahead of time.

Right now, we're seeing the impact of a decade's worth of silence and suspicion between the two countries. The current level of tension transcends that of the rough period after 1999 when Russia and NATO faced off over actions in Kosovo. Relations are even more jagged and mean-spirited now than they were in 2014 when Russia invaded Ukraine and illegally annexed Crimea. I believe this sad development stems in large part from the lack of contact between today's young and middle level U.S., Russian and European military and diplomatic personnel since 2014. It's much easier to demonize someone you don't know. The lack of contact takes on a potentially lethal aspect when you have military hardware, ships, aircraft, and ground maneuver units rattling sabers, conducting necessary assurance missions and posturing at each other across nearby borders and boundaries. If we're going to close the trust gap, we need to find credible ways to de-mystify and 'de-demonize' each other. In this spirit I remain involved in U.S.-Russia relations by participating in several "Track II" non-governmental U.S.–Russian exchanges and conferences where senior retired practitioners discuss the major issues—and opportunities—confronting the two nations and provide recommendations to their governments.

As this book goes to press, I can't overstate how much my early experiences in the U.S.S.R. and post-Soviet Russia colored my military service and worldview. A firm Cold Warrior in the past and an ardent NATO advocate today, I like to think these repeated early experiences of *"Swimming the Volga"* helped me get behind and beyond the official Russian persona to learn the value of balance, context, and empathy. After 32 years of direct contact with the Russians, I strongly believe that despite all the baggage, heartbreak, and mutual resentment, we have more in common with the Russians than not. Whether we feel or realize it yet, I believe we are going to need each other in very real ways in the next generation.

That said, I'll be frank and admit that I will never fully understand the Russians. Few outside of Russia ever will. Those of us who did not grow up there can never viscerally grasp the emotional impact of the nation's difficult history—a series of colossal tragedies in both war and peace that consumed so many families and loved ones. The impact of the world wars, revolution, famines, mismanagement, police terror, authoritarian leaders and more, left a deep scar on every Russian – and prior Soviet - family and on the nation as a whole. Awareness of this traumatic history can shed light on

Russia's often aggressive and reactive actions but should never be used to justify or explain them away.

One final observation about a glaring oversight in Swimming the Volga that I candidly admit to—one that spotlights just how opaque the Russian political process can be. In discussing the large field of candidates for the Russian 2000 presidential election, who did I fail to mention? Vladimir Putin! His rise during the late Boris Yeltsin years, followed by his win during that pivotal election, is a good reminder that Russian politics are not a straightforward exercise. My solace is that most Russia-watchers likewise missed his ascension.

The question today is will Putin remain in office with the prospect of his presidential term extending to 2030, or as far out as 2036—a real possibility? Or less likely, will we be dealing with someone new after 2024, whose view of the world might be quite different from Putin's? Did we end one Cold War, only to begin another? These are just a few of the pressing questions the world faces as we mark the thirtieth anniversary of the historic break-up of the Soviet Union.

By the Volga 1989.

With friends.

Bankrupt Tver Bank.

Early 1990s after the fall of the USSR ... major renovation and reconstruction ongoing of long-neglected Russian Orthodox structures such as the Cathedral of the Ascension in this picture.

Some of the 1989 American Students with teacher.

Winter 1993. With Russian artist showing off his Alsatian "puppy."

Remembrance of Igor on frozen bank of Volga, 1993. He is with his girlfriend, friend and with me in fur hat. His old friend gave me a picture of his distinctive gravestone that so captured his personality. He died from complications linked to alcoholism.

A humorous winter evening with some ex-Army Kalinin citizens. Note the vodka, likely procured from a back trunk of a taxi, was copiously flowing.

Older woman standing in front of the so-called "KGB villa" next to the Mednoye killing field where several thousand Polish officers were ruthlessly executed in 1940. As a child she remembered those terrible days.

Distinctive statue on south bank of Volga of Afanasy Nikitin, Tver's great explorer, who in 1469 was one of the first Europeans to open India.

Tver's main square with statue of Lenin still present. Adjacent is a common grave containing the remains of a large unknown grave of Soviet soldiers who died in the winter battles that enveloped Kalinin in winter 1941.

With friends standing by the jaunty statue of Russia's greatest poet and literary stalwart Alexander Pushkin, who often frequented Tver and the Volga region before perishing in a duel in 1837.

Kalinin's "beach," circa 1991.

OTHER VIEWS, OTHER VOICES

REMINISCENCES OF RUSSIA:
SIX CLASSMATES REMEMBER 1989 KALININ

One of the many pleasures of my stay in Kalinin was the chance to get to know my fellow students and more than a few Kalininites. Even after the official cultural program ended, I stayed in touch—or tried to—with many of the unforgettable characters I met that summer. I often thought about my Russian friends as I moved on in my military career. Occasionally I had the great luck to catch up with them in person on my travels; other times, I had to settle for news from mutual acquaintances; too often, all contact was lost and I was left wondering (and worrying) about where and how they were faring in a post-U.S.S.R. world.

I have included here two of my many letters home to family and friends written between 1990 and 1999. Like the main narrative of Swimming the Volga, the notes reflect the life and observations of a young U.S. Army officer and his family during the fast-changing world of the 1990s. Written 'in the moment', rather than retrospectively, these extracts capture a more immediate view of events .

More recently, I reached out to several of my fellow program participants from that summer and asked them to share their memories and thoughts about our experience in Kalinin. These talented individuals— some of whom carried on subsequently with Russia-related endeavors—offer their varied and very personal perspectives of Russia, then and today. Heartfelt and insightful, their comments capture the mix of optimism, hope and disappointment that many of us felt in the years after that extraordinary summer.

MAY DAY 1990

Dear fellow Kalininites,

Greetings from Garmisch-Partenkirchen, West Germany. Several apologies are in store here, first for my absolutely abysmal writing record and secondly for the total impersonality of a form letter. Sadly, I know myself all too well; the prospect of writing twenty or more individual letters was just simply too daunting a prospect for me. Okay, enough of the preamble.

It was truly a pleasure for me, as an at times insulated Army officer, to have met you all last summer. I had already been out of college for a dozen years when I met you. On the trip I learned not only plenty about the *Soyuz* but also a lot about what was happening on our campuses, including trends, beliefs, goals, politics, and interests. You certainly were an active, fun, and entertaining group; I'm much richer because of you all. I trust you all have had an interesting year, especially those of you who are budding Sovietologists. What a year it has been in the U.S.S.R. and Eastern Europe. At this time a year ago, the world geopolitically hadn't changed much since Yalta. Now Eastern Europe has completely been transformed and the U.S.S.R. is fighting for the political and social fabric of its society. Thinking back to Kalinin last year, how many of us could have read or anticipated the sheer breadth and scope of the changes which have occurred since then? We were all, I feel, cautiously optimistic about *glasnost* and *perestroika* from what we saw, the conversations we had, the contacts and friends we made. Through my limited view of Kalinin, it seemed that life there was depressing but livable, with enough food and clothing to get by without major hardship, though certainly without much choice.

Now, I just don't know. Much of what I've seen, heard, and read has been really troubling. *Perestroika* as a concept seems just about dead. The economy has fallen by ten percent, the CPSU (Communist Party of the Soviet Union) is in the process of breaking into opposing factions, the military is increasingly restless, the standoff over Lithuania could turn uglier, problems with the minorities and other restless republics, the rise of Pamyat, rampant crime, even less food, and products on the shelves and a public who is increasingly antipathetic towards

Gorbachev. Some say here the country is on the verge of civil war or at least civil breakdown.

I just returned last night from a ten-day swing through Moscow, Leningrad, and Riga with a group of twenty-five U.S. Army Russian Institute students. This was the first time back in Russia since my time in Kalinin, and it felt different, not radically so, but nonetheless perceptible. It seemed that everything was just more run down. *Glasnost* hadn't changed much since when we were there; however, the freshness and idealism of it all has faded. True, *glasnost* had in part brought on the beginnings of a representative political system (I will D.Q1 call it 'democracy'); however, that's about all. There is a lot of apathy on the streets, and the hustle for a buck or ruble continues at an ever more frenetic pace. The black marketing in Moscow is as I remember it before; however, beautiful, crumbling Leningrad has fallen under the control of various mafias, so much so that one cannot walk ten meters on Nevsky Prospect without somebody approaching you. It's so well organized that different groups control city blocks in Leningrad. One way to shake the most persistent is to keep walking until you can cross a street or avenue; most will peel off because they don't want to cross into another group's territory. There's a new twist in Leningrad: packs of grade school kids—obviously blowing off school—hustling as a group on the streets and working *Oliver Twist*-like for some older Faganesque character. The ruble rate is now six rubles to one dollar legally, a tenfold increase in legal buying power. The street rate is between ten and twelve to one, with the trader getting about fifteen to one with whomever he trades with.

Do you remember the Museum of Atheism in Leningrad? At night it has become the main center of political debate in the city. On any given evening before midnight, one will find knots of people arguing the issues, and now nothing is sacred, including Lenin. While I was there, I saw a Russian Navy Commander debating in one group, in another a Peoples Deputy. There were a half dozen of us, all Army officers, and just imagine the crowd reaction when they found out who we were. Many had never seen U.S. military before. Needless to say, before long, we were all in our own respective knots of debaters; I talked until I was hoarse for three hours. Types of questions being asked: What did we think of the situation in Lithuania; what did I think of the U.S.S.R.; of Bush, Gorbachev, and Yeltsin (who has not faded away); *perestroika*, etc. Most were quite friendly and open as we experienced in Kalinin, however, I feel there is an increasing mean-spiritedness on the streets, which could lead to big trouble in the near future.

One thing really interesting was my brief trip to Latvia. All are watching the ongoing Lithuanian succession drama closely, especially as the Latvians may be declaring their own independence this May. I can say this: Latvia looks, feels, smells, and tastes like its own country. The architecture is Germanic, the language different, the streets are cleaner, there is more food, and nobody wants to speak Russian. The language of choice was German. Also interesting about Riga is that the population is seventy percent ethnic Russian, many of whose families have been around for generations—and most of them also want out of the U.S.S.R.! Vilnius, in contrast, is eighty percent Lithuanian. Perhaps the largest issue concerning the Baltic States and Moscow is how they would treat their Russian minorities upon statehood. Stay tuned: the Baltic situation is far from played out!

I could regale you with more stories about this trip; however, frankly, nothing can match our summer last year in Kalinin. I am hoping to drop in to surprise some of our mutual friends there in the beginning of July and maybe, as per class tradition, take a dip or two in the Volga. My plans, tentatively, are to travel with two friends to Soviet Central Asia for several weeks in June and then finish up with several days in Kalinin. I will most definitely drop in on the University and also will try to find Laura and this summer's group. I will send anybody we met last summer your regards; if you have specific messages, let me know; I'll be taking off on June 2.

Enclosed for most of you are several pictures I hope you enjoy. If you have interesting photos you think I would like; please fire me off a copy or two. I'd really appreciate it as I've been compiling a photo album.

Also, with this letter, you have my address in West Germany. Garmisch is absolutely beautiful any time of year as it is nestled in the heart of the Bavarian Alps. I will be here until June 1991. I have two bedrooms in a house not far from the town center and needless to say, if your travels take you to the Munich area, you've got a place to stay. If you are thinking about dropping in, just give me some lead time.

A bit about myself. I'm heading into the third year of my language studies and still marvel at the difficulty of the Russian language. After graduation, it is very possible that I will become one of the inspectors involved in the mutual nuclear, chemical, and conventional weapons disarmament effort. If so, I will remain in Germany, from where I would take frequent trips to the U.S.S.R. Or, I may become a Company Commander (four hundred persons) in Sinop, Turkey, for one year at one of our 'radar' stations on the Black Sea. There is also a reasonable chance I could return to Washington D.C., a city I really enjoy. On the family side, things are exciting because my father is in the process of getting back a large chunk of the family business in Hungary, which was expropriated, *in toto*, in 1948.

I will most definitely be in New York for the Christmas holidays this year. If any of you are in the area, a reunion would be great fun.

To My "Kalininite" Comrades" (1993 Extract)

As I have been twice to Kalinin (Tver) since I last wrote, I thought I would update you on changes I've seen since our long summer together in the summer of 1989. First off, Tver has changed a lot, though the dusty city looks exactly the same. As an important provincial town, astride the main truck route between Moscow and St. Petersburg, it has plenty of big-city troubles. Tver has developed two economies like much of Russia, one based on traditional work morays, which means many barely live at subsistence level, and the second, the shadowy 'service industry', which means trading, profiteering, and speculation.

I continue to stay at the Motel Tver, on the edge of town, which has become a haven for the Finnish and Scandinavian truck drivers headed to and from Moscow. Many are a corrupt lot and work-trade deals on the side with the local Russians. At night, the Motel has been an interesting place to hang out. How many of you remember Dmitri, who used to loiter in a New York Giants jersey outside the University, trading rubles for dollars at eight-to-one? He now is one of the top speculators in Tver and owns a kiosk dealing in hard currency in the lobby of the Motel Tver. He mans it in twenty-four-hour shifts with several very attractive young ladies. He and I maintain the cordial relationship we had in 1989—he remembers me well as the guy who wouldn't trade currency, though I did collect a squad of various Russian military uniforms, which at the time was still a big deal. As this was my fourth time at the Motel, I've developed a good relationship with the desk person who made sure that the local criminal elements didn't hassle me.

I went back to the University several times. I feel like a valued alumnus there and saw all our old teachers. They were shocked to see me in winter as I had always been a summer visitor. Unfortunately, news was mostly bad. The academic exchange program and relationship, so laboriously built up by Laura and the Russians in 1989-1990, have fallen apart. No American group showed up last summer. Much of the squabble was about money (what else?) and who would host the Americans. Tatiana Aleksandrovna, the marvelous Russian founder of the group, is very sick with probable stomach cancer and could not lend her considerable energies to solving these problems. I saw her briefly; she can't weigh more than ninety pounds.

I also saw Svetlana, my Russian language instructor at Tver. This wonderful woman was realizing the dream of a lifetime; a trip to Paris in a delegation of Russian teachers (she taught French). Other than that, the news was glum. We talked at length about the serious problems affecting Russia and Tver. A teacher for over twenty years, Svetlana earned about 5,000 rubles a month, which was raised in January up to 14,000 rubles. (Her teacher's assistant earned 1,500 rubles!) Svetlana's whole family works, and like many Russians, they have enough to eat due to the small plot of vegetables they cultivate from their *dacha* on the edge of town. It is the produce from these humble plots which keeps many Russians off the street during periods of acute food shortages.

Svetlana remains the great humanist she always was. She still believes that life will be better though concedes more 'dark days' ahead for Russia. She supports Yeltsin and sees no alternative to him. Her young teaching assistant, a petite woman of about twenty-five years old, suddenly chimed in with a rather radical diatribe about politics, reform, the Jews, the U.S.—all negative, which really surprised me. Svetlana politely told her to shut up and we continued our conversation.

As of December 1992, representative prices in Tver were as follows. Remember the typical Russian salary at the time was between 3,000R-8,000R a month (450R = $1)

- 25R - loaf of bread
- 25R - kilo of potatoes
- 100R - 10 eggs
- 180R - scrawny chicken
- 400R - adequate sausage
- 700R - good sausage
- 28R - liter of gas
- 50R - bottle of good Tver beer (brewery just opened)
- 300R - local Russian vodka
- 700R - Stolichnaya vodka
- 3,000R - Smirnoff vodka (U.S. made)
- 7,000R - Compact disc

The local Russians have a saying: "We used to pay five rubles for a full bottle of vodka, now we pay ten rubles for an empty one!"

How many of you remember our excellent instructor Pyotr with the mane of gray hair? I ran into him early one morning and recoiled at the smell of his breath. He had become pallid and overweight and was stinking drunk just before teaching a class. He also was missing one of his front teeth. He was a sad sight to see considering he used to be 'Mr. Sensitivity'— urbane and very polished. Later I saw Igor Z., our old friend from sauna nights and midnight hockey games. He still works by the stadium but has graduated beyond stenciling sports jerseys and tie-dying clothes. He is a middle-level guy in a local import/export trading firm and still looks and drinks like Rasputin. While sitting in his inner sanctum, he opened his safe, which was full of U.S. dollars.

My arrival was, of course, a shock to everyone; as I am viewed as a trusted old friend, everything stopped, and out poured the vodka. I saw Igor drink a bottle and a half by himself the two times I saw him, which is why he will never be a very successful businessman. He later took me with his Armenian friend Rudolfo to the 'clubhouse' of some friends of his. It was really quite impressive. They had bought an old-style Russian house, and by hand, had turned it into a beautifully accoutered home. The traditional outhouse had been replaced by two well-appointed bathrooms and the owner had a well-organized office for his trading business. Downstairs they had a private bar, where when we arrived about a dozen guys were sitting around eating and drinking. One, a tough-looking former airborne type, an Afghantsi took great interest in my being military (I never keep it a secret). The owner was justifiably very proud of his club. This smooth guy looked like a page out of the L.L. Bean catalog, a real Russian 'preppy.' They were very friendly to me. Only later did I find out that he was the head of the toughest group of mafia in Tver and that the Afghantsi was his personal bodyguard.

Do you remember Igor's beautiful girlfriend Ekaterina? They broke up last year. Word has it that she moved to Moscow where she has become a high-priced call girl. The trio of Raisa, Larissa, and Anna still remain close. Larissa, the deep brooding English speaker, recently got married and is pregnant. Raisa and her husband Yuri continue to live reasonably well. Yuri paints decent decorative art which he sells in Moscow. He recently started painting the beautiful Russian black lacquer boxes which have become somewhat of a rage in Europe, and the U.S. Anna continues to study German and English. Beautiful, charming 'Olga from the Volga' met and married a Belgian who was studying in Tver two years ago. They now live in Brussels. Her best friend, tall Marina, I have already written about.

I also bumped into Ivan, the history professor with whom we went to Borodino in 1989. He is still an ardent Russian nationalist and advocates a return to the Czar. He is one who blames both Yeltsin and the U.S. for much of Russia's woes today. He firmly believes in a Greater Russia. As a full professor, his salary was 7,000 rubles a month which is about what a typical doctor or scientist is paid. No small wonder that we are afraid that many of Russia's scientific elite will sell out to third-world countries with a nuclear ax to grind.

It was a strange time to be in Tver. The city had an eternally gray hue; daylight didn't break until 9:00 a.m., and darkness came quickly by 4:30 p.m. I arrived on December 16, which is a historically important day for Tver. Over the forty-five-meter tall Soviet war memorial by our Volga 'beach' brightly burned Kalinin's eternal flame for twenty-four hours. It cast an eerie, oily, orange pall over the gray city and could be seen from many miles away. December 16 was Kalinin's day of liberation from the Germans who occupied the city from October to December 1941 during their drive on Moscow. The Volga bridges in Tver we knew so well were the only points the Germans managed to cross the Volga (by an audacious *coup de main* using captured Russian tanks). They withdrew after the 1941 winter Russian counter-offensive carved up the depleted German divisions in front of Moscow. (Of note: I met an old Wehrmacht Company Commander from the 1st Panzer Division which crossed the Kalinin bridges).

I met John N. while in Moscow. He had come to Tver last year in the hope of establishing an 'education exchange' business with Maxim S., many of whom you met as one of our student guides. John arrived, and over a half a year period fell out with Maxim. The issue, of course, was over broken promises and money. Maxim essentially did not fulfill his side of the bargain and stonewalled John for several months. This was somewhat of a shock for John, who had come to regard Maxim as a future and honorable business partner.

Fed up, John finally left Tver, moved to Moscow, and is

teaching at an elite school for young Russians. A Greenwich Village man with wonderful liberal values, John has given up on the Russians, as have most Westerners who live and work on the Russian economy, get paid in rubles, etc. I also had the great pleasure to see that great philosopher king, and former Rochester football offensive tackle, Adam Perry. He is living with some friends in a vast apartment complex in the Moscow suburbs. Also a teacher, and young idealist, the Russian experience has also soured him. His tales of daily corruption, crime, and just coping in Moscow are harrowing. Frustrated by the sheer pettiness and stress of daily Russian life, most of them are going back to the States.

I saw Cordelia Bowlus a few months ago. She has been in Yakutsk and having a great experience teaching English. Heather Leisk recently wrote to me about the very interesting year she spent in Kharkov. Roger Park was also in Moscow, and Kelly Szalkowski spent a semester in St. Petersburg. I've also been in touch with Brian Regli, who I saw two years ago in Liberec, Czechoslovakia, and Jim Rutherford, who now works for a think-tank in Washington, D.C. Finally, I spoke over Christmas to Janise Willy who is now happily married in Boston.

In closing this section, does anyone know the whereabouts of Victor Boldewskul?

Laura Janda

Prior to taking up her current position as a professor of Russian Linguistics at UiT The Arctic University in Tromsø, Norway in 2008, Laura Janda worked at the University of Rochester and the University of North Carolina in Chapel Hill. She is the author of numerous scholarly works, and you can read many of those and also find out much more than anyone would reasonably want to know about her at her website: http://ansatte. uit.no/laura.janda/.

In the days of the old Soviet Union, opportunities for American students to study abroad in Russia were very few and far between. Virtually the only program available, and certainly the most reputable one, was the program run by the Council on International Educational Exchange, or CIEE. Most American Slavists who studied in Russia in the 1970s and 80s did so in the city that was then called Leningrad, on the CIEE program which just recently celebrated its 50th anniversary. I was there myself in 1979 and later served on the executive board of CIEE for a number of years. In the late 1980s, CIEE got the idea to take what was then a rather bold move, namely to bring American students to a destination other than Moscow or Leningrad. The idea was that Moscow and Leningrad were not representative of the rest of the country and that there was a whole different Russia that Americans never had a chance to see in those days. I volunteered to embark on this experiment as a group leader for the first batch of students who would go to what was considered a provincial town. The host site was named Kalinin at the time, although later it regained its traditional name of Tver'.

Negotiations with the host university in Kalinin and arrangements for accommodations and other logistics were entirely unproblematic, perhaps partly because I did not have very high expectations after having spent a summer in Leningrad in 1979. There were greater challenges involved in finding a co-leader from the US and in selecting the group of students. My original co-leader from Brown University fell and broke her wrist on the ice that spring and was not able to join us so I had to find a substitute. Various irregularities involving cheating on exams and dubious information on financial aid requests also turned up during the admissions process.

Of course, there was one rather unusual application in the pile from a young army captain by the name of Peter Zwack.

Stories about American students engaging in risky behaviors while studying in the Soviet Union were legion at CIEE meetings. I figured that having Zwack along would be a good idea because he would be a little older, a little more mature, and well disciplined. He could be a role model for other students and help me keep them in line. While Zwack did not lack in adventurousness, he did indeed have a good influence on the group as a whole and I'm really glad that I made that decision.

I will offer just a few anecdotal vignettes and that can serve as snapshots of my experience that summer in the town of Kalinin that we now know as Tver'.

In the Soviet period, other communist countries were labeled "socialist-friendly" and there were bookstores across Russia and Eastern Europe dedicated to the purpose of making the friendship among such countries visible. Getting valuable books, such as major works of famous authors and reference materials like grammars and dictionaries was notoriously difficult. While the market was flooded with officially-approved books that towed the party line, everything else was issued in tiny print runs and reserved for sale among "insiders" or foreigners who could pay in hard currency at the special "Beriozka" stores. The one exception was the network of bookstores representing "socialist-friendly" countries. There you could find real treasures. The problem was a total disconnection between the target audience and the location: in Russian cities like Kalinin (Tver'), these bookstores contained books in every language of OTHER "socialist-friendly" countries: Polish, Czech, Bulgarian, etc., but not Russian. And in the same store in Prague, for example, they had books in Russian, Bulgarian, etc., but not Czech. So, books that were highly sought after and impossible to procure in Russia were collecting dust in Prague, while Czech books of value languished on the shelves in Kalinin. And the employees at these shops in both locations were just as much window dressing as the books themselves since almost nobody ever bought them. In 1982 in Prague, for example, I obtained an Academy Grammar of Russian that I never could have bought in Russia. And in Kalinin, I bought a fine selection of books in Czech, including a Czech translation of Arnold Lobel's Frog and Toad which I read to my children back at home until it literally fell apart.

Consumer products and foods especially were supplied in a very small range of options. For most of the summer, the only cheese one could find was kolbasnyj syr which I guess one should translate as 'smoked cheese', although calling it cheese at all is rather generous. To supplement the lack of variety, one had to go to the outdoor market rynok and hope to find something more offered there. One fine sunny day a middle-aged man had posted himself by the entrance of the market and was selling popcorn in little cones fashioned out of paper. Popcorn was a novelty previously unseen by most people who came to the market that day, and I recall overhearing the following exchange:

Customer: *What's that?*

Seller: *Corn*

Customer: *But how did it get like that?*

Seller: *That's a state secret!*

This rejoinder of the salesman echoed a hackneyed phrase that characterized the totalitarianism of the Soviet era. It was refreshing to hear it used playfully, indicating that things perhaps weren't as restricted as before. Perhaps the most memorable event of the summer was the reopening of a church that had been closed for several decades. Victor Boldewskul and I and some other students spent some of our free time trekking around town and the nearby region to take a look at what was left of former churches but were by then mostly dilapidated ruins. Victor somehow discovered that one of them was to be reopened and we showed up for the festivities. It was quite an event. Only the skeleton of the church remained, bare walls and no floor. The three-foot-high weeds that had surrounded the structure had been hastily mowed down and strewn on the bare earth inside, sprinkled with wildflowers. The most amazing thing to me was the presence of large metal objects that could not have been purchased or crafted for the occasion, namely several brass candle stands (almost four feet high, each with wells for several dozen candles) and a bell that had been hoisted to the tower above the entrance. Where did these come from? we had to ask. The locals told us that when their grandparents and others in the town realized that the church was soon to be closed, they snuck off with the bell and candle stands and buried them in their fields during the night.

Descriptions of where these objects lay hidden were passed down in secret from generation to generation, so it was easy to recover them when the time was right. After the opening liturgy, which was attended by a bishop, we were invited to a special meal where locals brought forth a dizzying array of delicacies, none of which were kolbasnyj syr.

At the end of the summer, back in my own living room, when I opened my suitcase to show my family what I had brought back, a large cockroach jumped out and scurried away. Thus, a little piece of Russia came to roost in my home, and for all I know, its descendants might still be there. I, however, have moved on.

Archpriest Victor Boldewskul

Rector, Holy Epiphany Russian Orthodox Church, Boston

Boldewskul was a fourth-year student at Holy Trinity Seminary in Jordansville, New York, when he joined the Kalinin summer program in 1989. He was ordained by the Russian Orthodox Church in 1999.

WHEN I HEARD ABOUT AN opportunity to study Russian in a historical yet provincial city for six weeks in the summer of 1989, I jumped at the opportunity. In Tver, then called Kalinin, American students were invited by locals to their apartments, experiencing full hospitality and long, thoughtful and sometimes lively conversations going through the night.

This would be my first of several visits to Russia. Like Peter, I witnessed how the changing economic, political and social landscape would affect those from below. Some navigated with grace and success, others fell to hard times, some left, but most persevered. The concept of hard times is relative. For Russians who experienced the Second World War, the collapse of the State and the devaluation of their life savings, a three percent contraction of the GDP doesn't represent hard times.

In *Swimming the Volga*, we are reconnected with friends

that we met, as well as educated locals who, like me at that time, saw a hopeful future as light was shining on the past and Russians were, on one hand, rediscovering their history, and on the other hand engaging with Western economic/political ideals for their future. It is a snapshot into Russian reality from below in a time of transition.

In June of 1989, *glastnost* and *perestroika* were in full swing. Papers such as *Argumenti I Facti* were questioning the Stalinist era, and in Tver, a second church (dedicated to the Kazan Icon of the Mother of God) was reopened, and a twenty-year-old Russian Orthodox seminarian from Jordanville, New York—a son of second-generation Russian parents—freely brought in scores of Orthodox spiritual literature to a population thirsting for such content. Plans were made for the restoration of more monasteries and churches.

The events of the 1990s, including shock therapy, the bombing of the parliament and the rise of the mafia economy, joined with a more aggressive American foreign policy including NATO expansion, the bombing of Serbia and the invasion of Iraq on false pretenses inevitably will change Russian perceptions of the

West and Western ideals. Today, the United States and Russia offer different commentaries on these and other events. I believe, however, that with more interaction on a personal level, much like our group had in Tver in the summer of 1989, we all can benefit by learning from each other and overcome the current tension.

Jim Rutherford

Rutherford moved to Washington, D.C., upon his return from Kalinin and has worked for several federal government defense contractors on projects linked to strategic arms reduction, non-proliferation, Ebola and other national security issues.

I ARRIVED IN KALININ IN summer 1989 as a new graduate from a public university in Ohio. My 'foreign' travel at that time was limited to Ontario, Canada, just an hour from my parents' house. I didn't know what to expect, so anything was possible!

As a lifelong student of history, and as an International Relations major with a Soviet Studies focus, I was prepared for lots of stern-faced, gray-wearing, anonymous Soviets, but found the opposite to be (largely) the case. The Russians I met were warm, caring, curious and non-judgmental. We talked openly among ourselves. I'm hopeful these friends learned from me only good things about Americans, with the possible exception that we couldn't come even close to keeping up with them in terms of alcohol consumption, ice hockey, and soccer.

As Peter mentions, we were curiosities to the locals. Westerners were rare in Kalinin at that time. Based on my gait and height, I stood out as a non-local, but the locals assumed I was *pri-Baltiki,* i.e. from one of the Baltic States. They were thrown off by my accent while speaking Russian: it was a combination of American plus the flavors of my two primary Russian language professors at that point: one a Ukrainian, the other a Bulgarian. So I had fun with it.

Together with our Russian friends, we had many vodka-fueled nights of conversation and cigarettes (Marlboros we'd purchased on behalf of our Russian friends, who were not permitted to enter the hard currency stores). I was one of the American students for whom studying was secondary; I was there for the experience. I especially enjoyed my daily forays with Peter around town and down to the Volga, with Peter walking barefoot in order to develop his 'Hobbit feet.' He also introduced me to some of his new friends who were veterans of the Soviet campaign in Afghanistan. This was heady stuff for a Cold Warrior like me! And then there were the weekend trips to Moscow and (then) Leningrad, and the unauthorized day trip to the Napoleonic battlefield at Borodino. All great memories that helped me to make sense of the vastness of Russian history and literature.

I always will remember the generosity of our Russian friends. One young man—one of the ubiquitous 'Sashas'— carried a really awesome rucksack. Toward the end of our time together, I disclosed my admiration for the rucksack, to which he responded that it had belonged to his grandfather, who carried it during the Great Patriotic War (World War II). In fact, his grandfather was wearing it at Kursk when he had one of his legs blown off. "But," Sasha said, "You should take it with you back to America!" Of course, I refused this incredible offer but, even with my attempts to be polite, I probably still hurt Sasha's feelings. I still wish I could have handled that situation better.

Our conversations with the locals were illuminating but little did I know people like my friends in Tver in only a few months' time would bring down the Berlin Wall and topple repressive regimes in Eastern Europe. Just two years later, they contributed to the dissolution of the Soviet Union.

I was surprised by these seismic shifts, but then again I really wasn't. The people I'd gotten to know in Kalinin were smart and yearning for 'more'.

Later in life, I took twenty-five or more trips to (now) the former Soviet Union, from Russia to Central Asia to Ukraine to the Caucasus. My experience in Kalinin in 1989 gave me the bona fides to get to know the people with whom I worked and recall the warmth of which they were capable. It remains one of the best decisions I ever made.

Heather (Leisk) Richfort

Richfort was a rising junior at St. Norbert College in De Pere, Wisconsin when she joined the Kalinin summer program. She graduated in May 1991 with a degree in International Studies. After a stint in corporate finance, she currently works for the U.S. Navy as a financial management analyst and environmental protection specialist.

IN THE SUMMER OF 1989, I joined a group of thirty-some other students of the Russian language for a two-month study abroad program. I felt like a country bumpkin seeing the big city for the first time. Me, from a relatively small town (Green Bay, Wisconsin), a small liberal arts college with no established Russian language major, joining a group of students from 'big' universities, many of whom were light-years ahead of me in actual language ability.

I had been drawn to the U.S.S.R. in high school; I had a social studies assignment to follow any and all news about another country over a period of time. The U.S.S.R. was 'easy'—one Premier after another was dying. The cool thing was that their language looked and sounded like secret code, with an alphabet similar to ours, but with backward letters! Then I took a Soviet

Politics college course and was hooked. I knew studying Russia and the Russian language was what I wanted to do!

My father, himself a Captain in the U.S. Army, was nervous for me as I prepared for my trip that summer. He was a Baby Boomer who was in high school during the 1962 Cuban Missile Crisis, and who had been trained in the Army to believe that the Soviets were our enemy. I, on the other hand, steeped myself in Hedrick Smith's book, *The Russians*, to try to understand the people I would meet.

There was something magical about the summer of 1989. There was a new feeling in the air: *glasnost,* or 'openness.' People felt free to express their opinions, to criticize government corruption, to demand political rights and were extremely curious to meet their first batch of Americans. Not only that but Americans who were trying to learn and speak 'their' language!

What I discovered that summer was a very friendly people, who wanted what we wanted: a decent living, a safe community in which to raise their children, the chance to enjoy life with friends and family and have some sort of social safety net for their elderly years. They were not the bogeyman we Americans had been taught to hate. The same was true for the Russians, in reverse, as they got to know us.

Two short months later, the Berlin Wall fell. Over the next decade, I spent roughly five years in the former U.S.S.R.; much of it in the Russian-speaking city of Kharkiv, Ukraine; some in Kurgan, Siberia; and almost three and a half years in Moscow working for multi-national firms. I made life-long friends and became the 'adopted' daughter of an elderly couple, both professors, who encouraged me to go on to graduate school.

I saw many changes over the course of the 1990s, some for better and worse, but during that summer of 1989, we knew we were witnesses to something that would alter the course of history.

BRIAN REGLI

Regli was a rising senior at Georgetown University when he joined the Kalinin summer program. He graduated the following year with a B.A. in Government and Philosophy. He also holds a Ph.D. from The Fletcher School of Law and Diplomacy at Tufts University. Regli is currently Chief Executive of Revere Suburban Realty in Huntingdon Valley, Pennsylvania.

THE UNABASHED EXUBERANCE OF 1989 has been replaced by the unbearable tension of 2018.

The hope for a radical change from historical patterns of warfare and discord at the end of the Cold War has disintegrated; older patterns of great power, unilateral nation-state behavior has re-emerged as the primary mode of policy, dimming the dreams that a global consciousness and common interest could emerge from the 'end of history.' Everywhere we look, there appears to be a resurgence of rivalries, failures to communicate on all sides and little motivation to break the dysfunctional cycle.

If we apply a strong dose of realism to our reading of human history, the undiminished force of self-interest among national elites should not surprise us. Neither should we be surprised by the corresponding institutional path dependence among politicians resigned to a status quo derived from confusion, fear, and bureaucratic inertia. Nation states will be nation states; superpowers will assert their perceived prerogatives, disrupting the peace and stability that a global approach to problem solving could have made possible.

The attendant sense of disappointment arises as tensions mount. As global powers return to more familiar historical patterns, a sense of fatalism emerges, further clouding the relationship between two countries—the United States and Russia—that have more in common than present political conditions would indicate.

Both countries have, at their source, a sense of individual and collective greatness derived from the Western tradition; history has demonstrated both countries can be a force for good in the world, in great part because of the generosity and creativity of their people. Both have been scared by the divisions of war, by acts of terrorism, by a territorially bound desire for security, and by a tendency to view their size and scale as their greatest source of strength. Both countries overreach in almost identical ways throughout history, and now both countries have turned to autocratic voices in an effort to tame restless bureaucracies and perceived threats.

Both countries are now effectively following an identical foreign policy. On our side of the shore, we have decided that America must come first, with muscular trade and military action leading a unilateral charge to maintain predominance among the nation states of the world, which implies a corresponding weakness that Russia, China, and others are now in a position to resist. Russia has made a clear and unambiguous policy decision: a weakened United States serves its interests. Between election hacking, military activity in the Middle East and growing alliances with China and others, Russia's leaders have smartly identified physical and social weaknesses that it can exploit at little cost.

In the midst of disappointment and increasing conflict, the memories of our collective experience from 1989 resound as a decidedly different narrative. At every step, our Russian hosts matched our exuberance to meet and come to understand each other. The attitudes, spirit and social interaction echoed commonalities, rather than differences. We made efforts to explain our history and attitudes, and—even across a student's linguistic limitations—we heard the echo of collaboration over competition. Our Russian friends clearly wished to absorb the economic and cultural success of the West, and we hoped to share that success within the context of a global community stretching beyond national frontiers.

These historically fragile moments lingered for long enough to allow a false sense of security to settle into the United States, then violently ruptured by the tragic events of September 11, 2001 and compounded by the global economic instability that followed. Our country melted down its gold statues in an effort to wage war while attempting to maintain an unsustainable plateau of economic privilege.

Meanwhile, most citizens of the United States were unaware of the constant struggle of system transition in Russia, the level of resentment arising in a proud country unable to find its role in this new historical epoch. The rise of the Homeland Security State in the U.S.—a post-9/11 phenomenon—had always been a practical reality in a Russia uncomfortable with multiculturalism and facing its own realities of terrorism and economic instability; sympathy could certainly be shared, but not at the sacrifice of Russia's own sense of geopolitical prerogative.

The divergence of these trajectories leads to our present dilemma: will we continue with the instability and power politics of the past, or find shared causes and history that can generate true balance and mutual respect? There is no magical 'reset' button that takes us backward to better times. We must return to the hard work of diplomacy, discussion and debate during a time when patience is thin and solutions appear difficult. Our leaders must spend time together talking rather than throwing recriminations and decide that the strength of one country cannot be derived from the weakness of the other. In that regard, I believe our experience in 1989 and the stories that Peter shares offer a crucial lesson: our interests and historical experiences are similar enough to offer a framework for shared understanding. We can get along, as we have in the past. We need to remember that, even in the most difficult times.

PAUL NARY

Nary was a student of Russian studies and political science at Hunter College in New York when he applied for the Kalinin summer program. He has focused on international health issues for more than twenty years and recently pursued graduate studies at the London School of Hygiene and Tropical Medicine. He is currently on special leave from UNICEF.

MY THIRTY-FIVE-YEAR ASSOCIATION WITH RUSSIA began in 1981, when I joined my classical ballet school trip to Moscow, to watch the 4th International Ballet Competition, to see a classmate perform and to visit Leningrad. … The trip left me curious and a quest to discover the 'real Russia' became a decades-long pursuit for me.

The 1981 trip, *glasnost, perestroika* and a steady stream of optimistic coverage of the U.S.S.R. during the mid- to late-1980s led me (and many others) to believe that democracy, the free market, and limitless opportunities surely awaited those willing to engage with a quickly transforming U.S.S.R. Believing that a knowledge of the Russian language would open doors, I begin studying Russian in 1987.

I had barely scratched the surface in my Russian studies

when the Kalinin State University summer program opportunity presented itself. The 1989 visits to Moscow, St. Petersburg and Minsk, followed by five-to-six weeks' study of Russian in Kalinin was an unforgettable opportunity to witness the U.S.S.R. in its final days, to meet Russians and learn about their lives and of course, to improve my still nascent Russian language skills. The trip left me even more curious about the country, the people and their language. ...

Post-Kalinin, I kept up a correspondence with the Tver Inter-contact Group, organizers of our summer visit in 1989. So, on March 7, 1992, having been married just three weeks, my bride Simi and I set off for our *medovi mesyats* (honeymoon) with open-ended tickets to Tver, where we were told "a safe, clean and secure apartment" awaited us. We had agreed to work for the Tver Inter-contact Group for a ruble salary, on the condition that a suitable apartment was provided rent-free. My goal was to get involved in U.S.-Russian business, although I had little idea what that really meant. Our mutual goal was to continue learning Russian, make friends and contacts and stay—who knew?—possibly many years.

We arrived in Tver on International Women's Day, March 8, 1992. … Due to 'unforeseen circumstances', (lifting of price controls, dissolution of the U.S.S.R., etc.) our apartment was not ready yet, so we were provided with a tiny bedroom in the apartment of a *babushka* (grandmother), Lukinichna, who did her best to keep us happy, despite periods of Cold War between her and Simi, whom she disapproved of because she: a) did not wait on me, serve me, or cook for me properly; b) looked like she was about twelve years old and not old enough to be married and c) talked back when admonished for her endless sins (a and b, above), plus not knowing how to make blini, not knowing how to wash clothing properly in Lukinichna's Soviet era washing machine, etc. Owing to lack of a suitable apartment, limited money and vague business and scant opportunities, our employment with TIG was short lived. …

After close to four months in Tver, we moved to Moscow, where we joined colleagues Adam, John, and Darryl, teaching at the Stankevich House school for elite Russian children. In Moscow, I was promptly introduced to one of the Principal's 'patrons,' an emerging oligarch, whose English language tutor I soon became. With my side job tutoring the oligarch, I earned a comfortable dollar wage, was provided with chauffeur-driven transport to the oligarch's office and benefited from an association that, in the context of other relationships established in Russia, taught me that the business environment in Russia was anything but easy, legal or safe.

Throughout our fourteen months in Russia, I kept coming back to the question: Is any of this legal? Does the rule of law function here? Is this a safe environment for business? The answer I received and surmised from Russians and expats from all walks of life was consistently "NO!" My naivety turned out to be my best defense: while I told Russians that I sought to engage in U.S.-Russian business, developing a network of contacts and friends that could eventually enable me to serve some interesting function, nevertheless, I had no idea what sort of business I wanted to work in. And I didn't really know the first thing about running a business.

One notable business-related exception came from my oligarch's suggestion that I could work for him as a PR man, earning a dollar salary, driving a good car and living in a nice,

Euro-standard apartment. This would have been in essence, the achievement of my stated goals, yet I could not get over the feeling that something was wrong with the picture being painted. Was it the Chechen gangster who tried to shake him down one morning in the middle of our English lesson in his office in the former NKVD headquarters? Was it my oligarch's stories of visiting his friends in prison in Siberia? Was it the strange collection of international 'partners' I was introduced to, from Germany, the United Kingdom, Ireland, and the U.S., who said little but who gave me a strange feeling that something was not on the up and up? Or was it the clientele and my oligarch's 'associates' at the Brooklyn steakhouse during our first dinner with them, where I had the distinct feeling I was a part of a *Godfather* movie?

To make a long story short, having just moved back to the U.S. in the Spring of 1993, my wife and I gave the oligarch and his mistress a tour of the country, but the tour was cut short when he decided he'd had enough of me—not smoking, being a small fish in a big pond, etc. I was saved from being led down a murky road to U.S.-Russian business by fate and by my just being myself, not wanting to be a slave and frankly, not really knowing what I was doing anyway.

Meanwhile, I swore I would never speak Russian, travel to Russia, reach out to Russians, etc. I was finished. The dream had reached its logical conclusion. As a Russian friend from Tver used to say, "Choose life." So, I did. And having dabbled in PR in Russia and the United States, I ventured into international PR in Washington, D.C. But the PR business was not a good fit. For example, when told I would be handling Russian oligarch Boris Berezovsky's account, I turned it down, a move not seen favorably in the PR business. I was soon looking for my next career.

Eventually, I made my way, with family in tow, to Geneva, Switzerland, to manage programs for UNICEF's Regional Office for Central and Eastern Europe/Commonwealth of Independent States. I supplemented my work by returning yet again to the study of Russian at the United Nations Russian Language School, earning the U.N. certificate of proficiency in Russian in 2013.

While working at the U.N. along-side governments and in partnership with non-governmental organizations (NGOs), I was challenged with the question: Would a free and open Russia ever emerge? Truly, the rise of Putin caused me to seriously question such hopes and, indeed, my own engagement with Russia. Some personal and macro events have pushed me toward a period of non-engagement with Russia in recent years.

For example, on a trip to Russia with colleagues in 2008, a few incidents brought home the notion that a new era for Russia had arrived:

1) On the train ride from St. Petersburg to Moscow, a Russian man seated near us, who had apparently overheard our boss's loud and lively cell phone conversation (in Spanish), addressed our Ukrainian colleague toward the end of the trip, saying in Russian, "You know, if there's anyone I hate, it's foreigners."

2) An elderly Russian fellow, standing at the bar of a restaurant where I had just concluded a business meeting with Moscow-based colleagues—in English —turned to me as we left the Moscow restaurant and said, plainly and angrily, "Yankee go home."

An attempted robbery on Nevsky Prospekt, in St. Petersburg, plus the snotty customer service frequently encountered on that 2008 trip, are par for the course in today's Russia. And I would also acknowledge that all of the above could probably have been avoided by not speaking English (or Spanish) anywhere and at any time, at least in public, an unwritten rule that I have always tried to follow while traveling in Russia. But for me, the 'clinchers' that told me that my engagement with Russia was, at best, going to be on hold for a while, were the annexation of Crimea, the fabricated war against Ukrainian separatists, Putin's rise to power and most of all, Russia's meddling in the recent 2016 U.S. Presidential elections.

And while one could easily say that this meddling by Russia is just a contemporary example of what nation states do— they act in their own best interests, they spy, they engage in *realpolitik*, so what is there to be surprised or shocked about?— nevertheless, I am personally finding it difficult to imagine going back.

At some point in the mid-1990s, Princeton University Russian scholar Stephen Cohen said that Russia would revert back to authoritarian rule (or words to that effect). I did not want to believe him at the time; I even scoffed at him for his pessimism and cynicism. However, it is clear today that he was right. My own belief is that Russia will remain under some sort of authoritarian rule for generations to come. Perhaps I was naive to have ever believed otherwise.

I still adore the Russian language. I admire the artists, musicians, dancers, writers and many other brilliant people I have met from that land. I respect the courage and tenacity of the Russian people, a people who have been oppressed for centuries. I cannot say whether I would be brave enough to demonstrate against the current regime on the streets of Russian cities today? But the country is still a huge part of my life. Our cats, who adopted us in Kenya and have recently made the journey to the U.S., all have Russian names: Misha, Rudy, and Pushkin, some of the artists who originally attracted my wife and me to Russia.

Were I given the chance to live and work there again, would I take it? I am not so sure anymore, but the temptation would be there. Still, I will be forever grateful for the experiences I had. And I certainly have no regrets.

CORDELIA BOWLUS

Bowlus was a rising senior at the University of Kansas when she applied to the Kalinin summer program. She received her B.A. the following spring and went on to earn a Master's degree from the same school. Today she is the Director of the McNair Scholars Program at the University of Wisconsin-Oshkosh.

BASKING IN THE SUN ON the banks of the Volga, our favorite Kalinin haunt on lazy, hot days in the Summer 1989, the cool waters glistening in the sunlight, drifting effortlessly past us—belying the rapidly moving current just below the surface—we were young, mostly twenty-somethings, adventure-seekers, ready to live life dangerously.

Not unlike the millennials of today who do not remember a time when there was no talk of Islamic jihadist threats, life before the Cold War was an abstraction for us. We came of age in the era of Tom Clancy thrillers, a time when kids called their arch-enemies "fucking commies". The world was black and white then: us versus them. By the time my fellow students and I entered our baccalaureate studies in the mid-1980s, most major universities had well-established Soviet and Eastern European

Studies Programs, run by seasoned Cold Warriors and Eastern European expats. In my experience, these professors could be divided into three basic groups: those who never tired of raging about threats of the 'evil empire'; those who wallowed in their sorrow over the demise of the Russian motherland; and, last but not least, those who preferred to mire themselves in the soft, nuanced inflection of the Russian language, having a strong preference for the Golden Age of Russian literature, when the likes of Pushkin and Chekov so eloquently penned the pulse of the empire.

At our pre-departure orientation at Brown University a few weeks before heading to Kalinin, it was clear from the get-go that this was not going to be your traditional study abroad. Fellow student Heather Leisk and I bonded on the first day, barely able to contain our excitement over the impending trip. As we sat in our room discussing what we should bring, both in terms of necessities and gifts, we began talking about the things we'd read that were hard to come by, things like laundry detergent, feminine hygiene products and, yes, jokingly at first, condoms. The AIDS epidemic was raging, and there was probably not a sexually active college student at the time who did not live in fear of contracting this brutal disease. We had all seen pictures and read stories of amazing people wasting away, dying miserable deaths. We also knew that AIDS had made its way into the U.S.S.R., but from all reports, denial and prudish attitudes towards sex made AIDS a taboo topic. What is more, condoms, the most effective preventive measure short of abstinence, were either unavailable or of poor quality.

On the eve of our departure, Laura and Lennard, the two professors leading our group, seemed uneasy, as we met to go down the list of do's and don'ts. Gorbachev's *glasnost* or 'openness,' which had made our study abroad possible, was still evolving. Yes, it was a lot easier to bring some formerly banned items into the country, but we did not want to push our luck… or did we? Up until that point, Heather and I had yet to share our plan with others in the group; nor did we have the slightest idea what Victor, our aspiring Russian Orthodox priest, had up his sleeve. We soon found out.

Laura had given Victor permission to pop the question: "Listen, guys, I've got one hundred Bibles I'd like to take with me as gifts. As you know, the U.S.S.R. is officially an atheist country and Russian Orthodox believers have suffered greatly over the years. I have a feeling I might run into some problems going through customs with an entire suitcase of Bibles, but if each of you stow a couple of copies away in your luggage, we should be able to get through without having them confiscated."

If memory serves me right almost all of us jumped at the opportunity to help, eager to test the waters: Just how open was the U.S.S.R. anyway?

"Anything else?" Heather and I looked at each other, not sure how to proceed on the heels of Victor's request without sounding sacrilegious. We mustered up the courage to share the news: We wouldn't need any help transporting the one hundred condoms we'd convinced a nurse at the Brown University Health Center to donate to our cause of AIDS education in the U.S.S.R., but we just want everyone to know that we were happy to share. Looking back, it was totally absurd. I don't think we ever gave much thought as to how we, with our limited language abilities, were going to broach the topic of AIDS, much less condom use, but the bomb was dropped. No one would forget Victor and his one hundred Bibles, nor us and our one hundred condoms, most of which served the purpose of protecting members of our group, engaged in short summer romances.

We arrived at the Hotel Volga in the provincial city of Kalinin in late June 1989, knowing that we were at a pivotal point. *Glasnost* was viewed skeptically by many Western observers. Was the U.S.S.R. on the trajectory towards becoming a democratic state, or was it just a matter of time before totalitarianism raised its ugly head again? What was to prevent a *putsch*? After all, our visit was overshadowed by the Tiananmen Square massacre which, in one short June day, snuffed out the hopes and dreams of thousands of Chinese students. In Europe, East Germany's Erich Honneker showed no interest in loosening the noose on his political power, much less the physical wall which snaked its way around West Berlin.

But for now, in this window of time, openness ruled in Russia, and we were welcomed by our hosts, both official and unofficial. In almost no time at all, it seemed everyone in Kalinin knew that the *Amerikani* were in town. Black marketeers eager for hard currency and small children peddling *znachki* (lapel pins) circled us like hungry sharks, but for the most part, ordinary citizens were just curious, eager to learn about us, desperate to try their knowledge of English out on some native speakers. I will never forget the man on the street who, lubricated by one too many, serenaded me on with "We All Live in a Yellow Submarine," the extent of his English limited to the words of the Beatles! I excused myself before he could launch into "You love me, ya, ya, ya."

Nor will I forget our *dezhurnaya*, whose job it was to keep watch over all those staying on our particular floor of the hotel— the keeper of the keys, a veritable security camera with a disarming smile of gold and silver teeth. For my roommate Heather and me, she was our *babushka* (grandmother), making us hot tea and plying us with ginormous, slightly mutated tomatoes from her *dacha* garden. With the nuclear meltdown in Chernobyl six hundred miles south of Tver only three years earlier, we secretly wondered if these tomatoes may have absorbed a few too many radioactive isotopes, a concern that nonetheless never prevented us from devouring them.

With our *dezhurnaya* ever-present, we also had a built-in language partner, extraordinarily important when you are in the country ostensibly to improve your Russian but stuck living in the same hotel as your American compatriots. It was in the presence of our *dezhurnaya* that I realized on the second day of our stay how truly lacking my Russian language skills were. I knew archaic words such as 'coach driver' but could not ask for an additional pillow for my bed without using a dictionary. Common everyday expressions such as *da net*, literally "yes no" but meaning something along the lines of "not really," left me baffled.

Our *dezhurnaya* gave us a sense of security, allowing us to commingle with Russians staying on our floor … like the time Heather and I attempted to converse with some Soviet officers as they dined in their room—cans of fish with heavy Russian rye bread, cucumbers and tomatoes, no plates just army knives and forks, a bit of vodka to wash it down, together with their memories of the Soviet-Afghan war which, after ten years of combat, had only recently come to an end, yet another hopeful sign that maybe, just maybe the Cold War was winding down.

The Soviet Union of 1989 did not feel evil, nor did feel like an empire. Infrastructure in disrepair, shops austere. But what

Russians lacked in goods and 'freedom' they made up for in education. As our circle of acquaintances and friends grew, we were often reminded of the pride Russians take in being *kulturni*, an all-in-one word for being educated, sophisticated and cultured. In spite of its many deficiencies, the Russian system cultivated a deep love of learning. In addition to the STEM fields, an abiding respect for language, literature, and culture prevailed. (On the other hand, real historical scholarship was problematic.) Being knowledgeable about literature and music was considered essential, a fact I was continually reminded of. Hardly a day went by that someone didn't comment on my name: "Ah, Cordelia! She was the good daughter in Shakespeare's *King Lear*." I would beam, proud to have such a noble name, but astounded that Russians could be so knowledgeable about one of Shakespeare's more obscure works when throughout my life, the best I could hope for from fellow Americans was a rather unflattering: "Now, that's a nice old-fashioned name."

Maybe it is a poor reflection on me, but I recall very little about my language classes that summer, other than that our instructors were extraordinarily patient with us. In accord with a placement test, our group was divided up into levels. I was by far not the most advanced Russian language student and tired rapidly from repeating words, trying to nail the hard and soft sounds to no avail, conjugating and declining, when all I really wanted was to be is out there talking to people, muddling my way through, picking up new vocabulary through context.

For the most part, Heather, who was advanced enough to make up for my inadequacies, was my steadfast partner in these adventures as we tried our Russian out on everyone from bus drivers to little old ladies selling raspberries at the market. Together we made friends with Russian students our age and were even invited on many occasions to their homes, something that would never have been possible in the old Soviet days. One of my most vivid memories is our trip to an important town hall meeting, during which the renaming of our host city was being hotly debated. With Stalin now officially a *persona non grata*, residents felt free to voice their desire to drop the name Kalinin, who was an early Bolshevik and later Stalinist, in favor the city's medieval name Tver. The mere fact that this was being discussed in an open forum gave us hope that the barometer was pointing in the direction of a fledgling democracy. It was during that meeting that Heather became the center of attention when she stood up to voice in broken Russian her growing annoyance with the black marketeers to whom law enforcement turned a blind eye. The locals trying to eke out an honest living applauded her courage.

And, of course, there was our 'beach' on the Volga. Beautiful young Russian girls in bikinis basked in the sun, the most memorable of which was the young lady we referred to as 'Olga from the Volga'. As the Volga flowed past us on those hot summer days, we threw caution to the wind, wading ever deeper and ultimately challenging each other to traverse the river. There was danger in swimming across the Volga. It was illegal. River patrols would regularly speed up and down the river. But, perhaps most alarmingly, by the time the waters of the Volga reached our Kalinin, they had swelled with the confluence of the Tverska River, expanding the riverbed width to three hundred meters. Our prefrontal cortex not yet fully developed, we dove in anyway, swimming steadily, diagonally across, with the current, always landing at least one hundred meters farther downstream than where we had begun. Swimming in that ancient river—that artery connecting the Russian motherland to the Caspian Sea—we were small and vulnerable; the rush of adrenaline, wicked. We were part of something far bigger than ourselves.

For better or worse, after that summer, there was no going back to the way things were. Only a few months later, on November 9, 1989, the Berlin Wall would burst like a dam unable to hold up against the flood of raw human emotion. Eight months later, on July 17, 1990, Kalinin was officially rechristened Tver, signaling as much the end of the Bolshevik experiment as a return to the city's historical roots. By New Year's Eve 1991, after an ever-so-brief August Coup, the Soviet Union was no more. Fifteen of its Republics became independent states. The euphoria that followed was quickly replaced by deep disillusionment as black marketeers and their likes turned to organized crime or, calling themselves *biznessmeni,* sought out international companies with which to form joint ventures, often shady deals featuring the exploitation of Russia's natural resources. Completely unregulated, Russia's fledgling democracy was a metaphorical Wild East, where ordinary citizens, as *kulturni* as they were, struggled to make ends meet, hiding behind locked doors, fearful of break-ins and extortion, wishing they could swim back in time to a place when there was stability, maybe even a strong hand to keep order.

ACKNOWLEDGMENTS

AND IN CLOSING, A MOMENT of introspection and heartfelt appreciation to the memory of the late Leslie "Les" Gelb (1937-2019) who passed away before this book was published. He was a true Soviet-Russia hand from his over five decades serving our nation as a Pulitzer Prize winning journalist, at senior levels of both the State and Defense Departments, and later as President on the Council on Foreign Relations - who late in his retirement as its President Emeritus became an insightful and patient mentor to me on Russian affairs.

No earnest book can be written without acknowledging those most helpful to its publication. As such, I want to single out Ms. Terri Beavers, a dear friend of thirty-four years who tirelessly and mercilessly pressed me to publish this little volume, while doing much of its organization and designing.

Additionally, thanks must go to Kathi Ann Brown of Milestones Historical Consultants (https://milestonespast.com/) for her superb editing work. It's great to have a historian as an editor who can read much of the author's mind. And a big thank you to Clark Kenyon (https://www.camppope.com/) who engineered the layout of the book with an eagle's eye precision.

Most of all I want to thank my beloved and ever-patient wife Stephanie and my three children, Broghan, Peter Jr. and Alessandra, who I have dragged all over the world on quite a number of familial adventures, including two years in Moscow. Without them, I would be bereft.

To close, I must highlight those in my military profession, past and present, who have shown me the way throughout my thirty-four-year career. Whatever success I achieved could not have been attained without the great efforts, teamwork, and patience of those I soldiered with, whether bosses, peers, or, most importantly, those stalwarts who worked for me. These include those I deployed with as brothers and sisters in combat zones such as Afghanistan and my merry band of fellow Foreign Area Officers that decades ago broke down the doors of Cold War convention in their zest to travel and experience the East.

About the Author

RETIRED U.S. BRIGADIER GENERAL
PETER B. ZWACK

with Stephanie Zwack

BORN IN CHICAGO AND LATER becoming a native of New York City, Zwack went to the Latin School in Chicago, the Fessenden School in West Newton, Massachusetts, Trinity School in New York and the University of Denver. He then worked in Florence, Italy in the Italian wine business before joining the U.S. Army as a Private First Class in 1980.

After attending Officer Candidate School (into which he was inducted decades later into its Hall of Fame), he was commissioned to Second Lieutenant in 1981. In 1988, he was selected to become a Russian Foreign Area Officer (FAO). After a year of studying at the Defense Language Institute in Monterey, California, Zwack—then a young Army captain—was granted permission to attend a summer program with American college students at Kalinin State University—a rare opportunity for a U.S. military officer to study in the provincial Soviet Union. By then, Zwack was a specialist in the Soviet military and its strategy and tactics, a subject that defined his Army career and ultimately led to his assignment to Moscow as the senior U.S. Defense Attaché to Russia during the challenging 2012 to 2014 period.

During his many visits to Tver, Zwack's openness, his desire to understand Russian culture and his knowledge of Russian history gained him the trust of his new friends—so much so that on one occasion he was invited to visit a local polling station during the critical 1996 presidential elections, a gesture unheard of under the old Soviet regime.

Zwack's travels in the U.S.S.R. and within Russia during his long career included not only Tver but forays throughout the Far East, Central Asia, Caucasus, Siberia, and the Far North. One particularly memorable trip in 1991 involved a long, adventure-filled drive from Moscow south to Tblissi, Georgia with a fellow Army friend just before the break-up of the Soviet Union.* He also returned to Tver several times during his military assignment in Moscow from 2012 to 2014, and most recently in 2017.

In June 2014, during a period of significant tension, presenting a lecture in Moscow to an audience of Russians about WWII D-Day, our Normandy invasion, and the opening of the Second Front.

With Ambassador Michael and Donna McFaul, and my wife Stephanie standing in front of Spaso House in 2013 for its well-attended 4th of July celebration.

At Stalingrad's (today's Volgograd) in February 2013 laying a wreath with Ambassador Mike McFaul on the occasion of its 70th anniversary of the USSR's decisive victory over invading Nazi and Axis forces. Close to half a million Soviets perished in its epic defense.

In 2013 at a Russian commemorative event for WWII

With Colonel General Vladimir Zarudnitsky during official late autumn 2012 visit in Saint Petersburg.

At the Russian General Staff Academy in Moscow escorting in 2012 Lieutenant General Mark Hertling Commander of US Army Europe. This was a time when efforts were still ongoing to maintain cooperative relations between the US and Russian militaries.

END NOTES

1. Hungarian Wine House, http://www.hungarianwinehouse.co.uk/das-ist-ein-unicum/

2. Peggy Lohse, "Sandwiched between Moscow and St. Petersburg: How to spend a perfect weekend in Tver," Russia Beyond, March 7, 2018, https://www.rbth.com/travel/327745-travel-moscow-st-petersburg-tver-volga-perfect-weekend

3. "Battle of Bortenovo: 22 Dec. 1317," Xenophone International, http://www.xenophon-mil.org/rushistory/battles/borten.htm

4. Ajay Kamalakaran, "From Tver to Calicut: Retracing Afanasy Nikitin's Life in India," Russia Beyond, August 5, 2016, https://www.rbth.com/arts/history/2016/08/06/from-tver-to-calicut-retracing-afanasy-nikitins-life-in-india_618137

5. Irina Osipova, "8 Facts about Catherine the Great's Imperial Palace in Tver," Russia Beyond, January 26, 2017, https://www.rbth.com/arts/2017/01/26/eight-facts-about-catherine-the-greats-imperial-palace-in-tver_689378

6. Russiapedia, https://russiapedia.rt.com/prominent-russians/art/savva-morozov/

7. [Subscription required] Review of "The Defense of Moscow: The Northern Flank," Jacky Radey and Charles C. Sharp, Stackpole Military History, January 16, 2013, https://secondworldwaroperationsresearchgroup.wordpress.com/2013/01/16/book-review-the-defense-of-moscow-1941-the-northern-flank/

8. Tver State University, http://university.tversu.ru/en/general/history/

9. "Founder of MMM, biggest Ponzi scheme in Russia's modern history, dies in Moscow," RT.com, March 26, 2018, https://www.rt.com/business/422408-mavrodi-founder-mmm-pyramid-dies/

10. "The Most Notorious Barracks," Strelka, February 6, 2017, https://strelka.com/en/magazine/2017/02/06/the-most-notorious-barracks

11. "The Most Notorious Barracks," Strelka, February 6, 2017, https://strelka.com/en/magazine/2017/02/06/the-most-notorious-barracks

12. "The Most Notorious Barracks," Strelka, February 6, 2017, https://strelka.com/en/magazine/2017/02/06/the-most-notorious-barracks

13. "Zhirinovsky: Russia's political eccentric," BBC News World Service, March 10, 2000, http://news.bbc.co.uk/2/hi/europe/667745.stm

14. Michael Specter, "The Wars of Alexsandr Ivanovich Lebed," New York Times, October 13, 1996, https://www.nytimes.com/1996/10/13/magazine/the-wars-of-aleksandr-ivanovich-lebed.html

15. Lawrence K. Altman, "Yeltsin Has 7-Hour Heart Surgery and Doctors Say It Was a Success," New York Times, November 6, 1996, https://www.nytimes.com/1996/11/06/world/yeltsin-has-7-hour-heart-surgery-and-doctors-say-it-was-a-success.html

16. "File:4. Tver Church of White Trinity" (photo), https://commons.wikimedia.org/wiki/File:4._Tver._Church_of_White_Trinity._1787-1860.JPG

17. "File:4. Tver Church of White Trinity" (photo), https://commons.wikimedia.org/wiki/File:4._Tver._Church_of_White_Trinity._1787-1860.JPG

18. Anne Applebaum, "How Stalin Hid Ukraine's Famine from the World," The Atlantic Monthly, October 2017, https://www.theatlantic.com/international/archive/2017/10/red-famine-anne-applebaum-ukraine-soviet-union/542610/

19. Laura Hill, "The Great Purge of Stalinist Russia," Spring 2013, HI102 The

Emergence of Modern Europe, Guided History, Boston University, http://blogs.
bu.edu/guidedhistory/moderneurope/laura-hill/

20. "1999: NATO bombs Yugoslavia," This Day in History, March 24, 1999, History
Channel, https://www.history.com/this-day-in-history/nato-bombs-yugoslavia

21. "The Battles of Borodino: Coming Soon to a Field Near You," The Moscow Times,
August 29, 2017, https://themoscowtimes.com/articles/the-battles-of-borodino-
coming-soon-to-a-field-near-you-58789

22. "Russia Posts Katyn massacre documents online," The Guardian, April 28,
2010, https://www.theguardian.com/world/2010/apr/28/katyn-massacre-russia-
documents-web

23. "Love Tyrannises All the Ages: The Decembrists of Siberia," http://www.
nomadom.net/russia/decembrists.htm

24. Cnaan Liphshiz, "Liberal Jewish politician emerging as main opposition
challenger to Putin," The Times of Israel," January 19, 2018, https://www.
timesofisrael.com/liberal-jewish-politician-emerging-as-main-opposition-
challenger-to-putin/

25. "The Russian Crisis 1998: Economic Report," RaboResearch, RaboBank,
September 16, 2013, https://economics.rabobank.com/publications/2013/september/
the-russian-crisis-1998/

26. "The Russian Crisis 1998: Economic Report," RaboResearch, RaboBank,
September 16, 2013, https://economics.rabobank.com/publications/2013/september/
the-russian-crisis-1998/

27. "Blood Brotherhood: Chechen Organized Crime," Mark Galeotti, In Moscow's
Shadows: Analysis and Assessment of Russian Crime and Security, September 1,
2008, https://inmoscowsshadows.wordpress.com/2008/09/01/blood-brotherhood-
chechen-organised-crime/

28. "Palekh," Artrusse, http://www.artrusse.ca/palekh_en.htm

29. Andrew E. Kramer, "Yevgeny Primakov, Former Russian Premier and Spymaster, Dies at 85," New York Times, June 26, 2015, https://www.nytimes.com/2015/06/27/world/europe/yevgeny-primakov-former-premier-of-russia-dies-at-85.html?mtrref=search.tb.ask.

30. Joshua Keating, "Luzhkov's Russia? How the Disgraced Former Mayor of Moscow Paved the Way for Russia's Seizure of Crimea," Slate, March 5, 2014, http://www.slate.com/blogs/the_world_/2014/03/05/yury_luzhkov_how_the_disgraced_former_mayor_of_moscow_paved_the_way_for.html

31. "Viktor Chernomyrdin obituary: Yeltsin's protege and the longest-serving Russian prime minister of modern times," The Guardian, November 3, 2010, https://www.theguardian.com/world/2010/nov/03/viktor-chernomyrdin-obituary

32. Andrey Pertsev, "Sergei Kiriyenko: The Dreamer in the Kremlin," Carnegie Moscow Center, February 11, 2016, http://carnegie.ru/commentary/65015

33. Hassan Abbas, "Who Exactly Is Sergei Stepashin?", Prism, Vol. 5: Issue 10, May 21, 1999, The Jamestown Foundation, https://jamestown.org/program/who-exactly-is-sergei-stepashin/

34. "Peter Zwack," Pell Center for International Relations and Public Policy, http://pellcenter.org/peter-zwackcom&gwh=B6F9D2284D570D198197CBB455EC5136&gwt=